Fun-Filled Parenting will make you smile. Don't give up on the fun-factor—it's magical! You and your kids will be storing up fun, clever and silly memories for life. Believe me, Silvana lives her words and makes life a fun adventure for her family.

Dr. Barb Brock
Author of *Living Outside the Box*

• •

Fun-Filled PARENTING

A GUIDE TO **LAUGHING MORE** AND **YELLING LESS**

Silvana Clark

Regal

From Gospel Light
Ventura, California, U.S.A.

Published by Regal
From Gospel Light
Ventura, California, U.S.A.
www.regalbooks.com
Printed in the U.S.A.

Published in association with the literary agency of Janet Kobobel Grant, Books &
Such Inc., 52 Mission Circle, Suite 122, PMB 170, Santa Rosa, CA 95409-0537.

Library of Congress Cataloging-in-Publication Data
Clark, Silvana
Fun-filled parenting : a guide to laughing more and yelling less / Silvana Clark.
p. cm.
ISBN 978-08307-4795-5 (trade paper)
1. Parenting. I. Title.
HQ755.8.C53 2007
649'.1—dc22
2006102727

1 2 3 4 5 6 7 8 9 10 / 19 18 17 16 15 14 13 12 11 10

Rights for publishing this book in other languages are contracted by Gospel Light
Worldwide, the international nonprofit ministry of Gospel Light. Gospel Light
World-wide also provides publishing and technical assistance to international
publishers dedicated to producing Sunday School and Vacation Bible School
curricula and books in the languages of the world. For additional information,
visit www.gospellightworld wide.org; write to Gospel Light Worldwide,
P.O. Box 3875, Ventura, CA 93006; or send an email to
info@gospellightworldwide.org.

To order copies of this book and other Regal products in bulk quantities,
please contact us at 1-800-446-7735.

Contents

Acknowledgments

· ·

Without my husband, Allan, our family would be pretty boring.
He's the one who comes up with all the creative and
off-the-wall ideas that make our family fun.

Thanks also to my two amazing daughters, Trina and Sondra,
who cheerfully go along with all of Allan's wild ideas.
What a team!

A special thanks to my editor, Kim Bangs,
who understood my idea for a book that showed
the lighter side of parenting. Now, Kim, we just
have to get you to New York to experience
those Broadway shows!

Introduction

● ●

But the fruit of the Spirit is love, joy, *peace, patience,*
kindness, goodness, faithfulness . . .

GALATIANS 5:22 (EMPHASIS ADDED)

It looked like the typical scene taking place in airports across
the country.

"But I don't want you to leave, Mommy!" wailed my four-
year-old daughter Sondra. I reassured her (to no avail) that I
would only be gone on my business trip for two days. "Please,
please don't go!" she continued, clutching my leg for extra theatrical effect.

As I tried shaking her off my leg, Allan, my husband, said,
"Sondra, come here so I can tell you a secret plan about what
we'll do when Mom is gone." She hesitantly went to him as he
made a grandiose show of whispering to her. Within seconds the
tears disappeared as she clapped her hands and jumped up and
down, yelling, "That's a great idea, Dad! It's a fantastic idea!" She
skipped off with Allan, not even bothering to say goodbye.

Two days later, I walked off the plane into the waiting area,
looking for Allan and Sondra to take me home. Instead of seeing my husband and daughter, I was greeted by Dorothy and
the Scarecrow from *The Wizard of Oz.* Allan's "secret plan" was
to use the time I was gone to make costumes to wear when they
picked me up. Allan, in bare feet, overalls and a straw hat, kissed
me, as "Dorothy" clicked her sparkly red shoes while clutching
a stuffed Toto.

"We made costumes," she explained. Yes, indeed. I could
tell instantly that they had spray-painted her shoes red, then
dumped glitter over the damp paint. Allan's costume included

straw poking out around his neck and from the sleeves of his plaid shirt. Later on he explained, "Sondra and I have a new tradition. We're going to make different costumes every time we pick you up from the airport." He went on to say he wanted her to learn creativity in problem solving. Sondra missed me when I traveled, but the solution was to use the time apart for designing costumes and teaching her to have a joyful spirit.

For the next two years, Sondra never cried when I left. In turn, I was greeted by a host of characters at the airport. There was Christine and the Phantom of the Opera (complete with half a mask covering Allan's face), and Peter Pan and Captain Hook. Another time I arrived to see two characters straight out of *Grease*: Sondra looked adorable in her ponytail and poodle skirt while Allan was every bit the thug with slicked back hair and a tight white T-shirt.

We've come to call those airport experiences the beginning of *Fun-Filled Parenting*.

Most of us receive training at work for how to create a spreadsheet or set up a window display. As adults, we need additional training when it comes to being a parent. Have any of us ever held our first tiny newborn baby and said, "Oh, this will be a breeze. I know everything there is to know about raising children"? More likely, most of us hold that tiny baby and feel overwhelmed at what to do in the next 30 seconds when the baby cries.

Consider this book your parenting training guide, your handbook for learning what joyful adults do to raise happy children.

Perhaps you're skeptical about reading yet another book on "how to" parent. Maybe you think parents who dress in costumes at the airport need to be sent to traditional parenting classes. But trust me—parenting *can* be fun, and you don't want to miss out on anything. So keep an open mind and read on.

Consider one mom who found herself getting in yelling matches with her headstrong daughter. She decided to take a community parenting class, and that decision to get some guidance made all the difference. "That instructor gave one tip that changed my life," she said. "I learned that I needed to use adult behavior when dealing with my daughter instead of acting like another preteen. The instructor suggested we pick an adult we really admire and when things get heated, talk to our children the way our role model would. I have always admired Katherine Hepburn for her strength and composure. Now, when my daughter starts getting upset with me, I simply pretend I'm Katherine Hepburn and talk to my daughter in a calm yet powerful voice. It works! I no longer get into petty arguments with my daughter—and I think I'm due an Academy Award for my amazing dramatic skills."

So what's the Fun-Filled Parenting philosophy anyway? *To parent effectively and to have fun while you're doing it.* Sometimes that means acting like Katherine Hepburn and sometimes it means playing Beach Boys music while folding laundry with your children.

Instead of posting a list of household rules with appropriate punishments on the refrigerator, make a list of low-cost, easy-to-do activities that can be done in 10 minutes or less. Just having uninterrupted fun with your children for a few minutes after school can result in less stress the rest of the night. Why not celebrate National Twinkie Day, go on a spontaneous car trip, or mix up a batch of homemade play dough? You're almost certain to have a home in which family relationships are strong and everyone feels comfortable laughing together.

Where do you get that list of activities? Simply glance through this book and you'll see hundreds of practical ideas. Pick and choose what seems to work best for your family. Don't be afraid to experiment. If your family has never volunteered together, offer to walk dogs at the local Humane Society. Not very crafty? Spend 10 minutes making paper sculptures that even a three-year-old can do well. The idea is to get beyond watching TV together while calling it "Quality Family Time."

And lucky for you, you don't have to pay a high-priced professional to give you some parenting tips. Just start reading this book and see how easy it is to get your family smiling, exercising, reading, creating, baking, walking, exploring, joking, dreaming and laughing—together. (And don't forget the costume-making!)

1

Let's Get Silly with Our Kids

He will yet fill your mouth with laughter.

JOB 8:21

We've all watched in shock as children on a nanny-related TV show run through their house, kicking the dog and pinching the baby. The children's parents roll their eyes in frustration, moaning, "I can't handle my kids."

Then, striding through the front door, comes a professional nanny, ready to do a complete makeover on their parenting techniques. She doesn't come alone. Oh, no. A whole camera crew camps out in the home for a week, documenting all the parental follies.

But never fear: By the end of the hour-long television show, the nanny has brought the family completely under control. The children now eat at the table, use "inside" voices and share their toys. The biggest revelation is for the parents, who say, "Nanny suggested we spend more time doing things with our family. She set up specific schedules for us to do an activity together. Just spending time having fun has helped our family tremendously."

There's no guarantee your children will be transformed into angels after a game of UNO. The odds are in your favor, though, that discipline problems will diminish in direct proportion to the amount of time you and your child spend doing things together. Don't worry—I'm not suggesting you take weekly trips to Disneyland. But you might consider a weekly family trip to the library or a walk around the block as you search for unusual stones.

Only a few families are selected to appear on TV with a professional nanny at their side. The rest of us need some ways to enjoy our family that use our own God-given creativity and resourcefulness.

The Funny List

In our family, the greatest honor is to get your name on "The Funny List." Being on the honor roll, earning a raise or winning a national award as an author is inconsequential when compared with the honor of having a family member say, "Congratulations, you made The Funny List!" My husband and I know that having a positive and upbeat attitude about life is more important than knowing the main export crop of Peru (which, by the way, happens to be asparagus).

Back to The Funny List. Several years ago, we decided our family needed more levity. We needed gut-busting belly laughs and ordinary chuckles. Thus, The Funny List became a badge of honor with our family. The rules are simple: Do something incredibly funny that makes the rest of the family (or anyone else) laugh until their eyes water. The event is then ceremoniously recorded on The Funny List.

One of my favorite Funny List incidents took place when our family took a three-hour Mystery Dinner train ride. While eating dinner, actors came by our table, acting out situations and leaving clues. At the end of the evening, everyone received paper and pencil with instructions to write an ending to the plot, solving the mystery. Not feeling very creative, I didn't participate.

Soon, the winners to the Murder Mystery Story Contest were announced. A perky staff person announced the first place winner: Silvana Clark. *What? I hadn't even turned in an entry!* The hostess had me stand as she commented (to me and everyone else in the room), "Silvana, you must have some romantic thoughts going through your mind to write a story like this." *What is she talking about?* The hostess then began reading the story in her most melodramatic way: "Lillian, worn out from running away from Paul, could only think of her love for Michael. With every beat of her heart, she knew Michael was the only man that could ever satisfy her passion for true love." The story continued like some amateur Harlequin romance. The audience in the train car howled at the soap-opera-esque plot line and romantic innuendos.

It was then that I looked over at my smirking 15-year-old daughter. With a huge smile, Sondra said, "Now *that* makes The Funny List." She had written the story filled with pathos and passion—and then signed my name. Yes, she had made The Funny List, a great honor indeed.

Just last week, our family enjoyed a visit to New York. That evening in the hotel room, Allan asked for some Hershey's kisses. I quickly tossed a handful at him, one at a time, as he tried in vain to catch them. He reached underneath the dresser to retrieve a piece of chocolate. "What is this?" he asked, holding what looked to be a Tootsie roll. No, it wasn't an old piece of candy but a piece of petrified dog poop. Allan immediately proceeded to chase Sondra and me around the room with his smelly find.

That rated an entry on The Funny List. Pretty juvenile humor? Maybe. Inexpensive fun? Yes. It sure beats sitting comatose in front of the TV and calling it "family time."

Best of all, it made The Funny List.

Enjoy the Gift

Christians are always told, "Children are a gift from God." We all enjoy gifts, so why is it we forget to enjoy our children? There is nothing wrong with a spontaneous pillow fight or even a burping contest. There's more to raising children than making sure they clean their room and eat a healthy diet. Think what it would be like if we concentrated on developing a warm, close relationship with our children.

Children need a light-hearted atmosphere at home. Don't feel overwhelmed, thinking that you need to develop a nightly comedy routine or wear a clown outfit to entertain your kids. Each chapter in this book has a gradual, month-long approach to making some positive changes in your home. Why not start by trying Silvana's Four-Week "Let's Get Started Having Fun" program?

Silvana's Four-Week "Let's Get Started Having Fun" Program

Week One

Read some funny books or magazines together. What easier way to add some fun to your family than simply reading out loud? Go to the library, a bookstore or even the Internet and find humorous material. Then, instead of sitting in front of the TV, sit around the fireplace and read aloud—and laugh!

Don't have a fireplace? Make that part of the evening's activity, by drawing flames on a piece of cardboard and taping it to the wall. Yes, your children will wonder about your senility, but they'll also delight in laughing together.

Read three jokes and vote which one is the funniest.

If nothing else, read the comics together with your family.

Week Two

As a family, make a list of positive family memories. Write down silly things that have happened, such as the time when the hamster got loose and ended up in Mom's underwear drawer. Now get ready for the big event in your life: starting your own Family Funny List. Label a piece of paper "The Funny List" (creative title isn't it?). Explain the honor and prestige that come with doing something so funny that it is recorded on the infamous List. Place the list in a safe location and wait to see whose name appears first.

Week Three

This week requires some work on the part of parents. Come up with two activities for the family to do together. Remember, they don't have to be grandiose and expensive. Helping your children decorate the driveway with sidewalk chalk counts as an activity. To help you out, here are some ideas:

1. Give everyone solid-colored placemats from the Dollar Store. Have each family member decorate his or her placemat using permanent markers.

2. Take a walk after dinner, even if it's dark or rainy (that only adds to the novelty!).

3. Play a game of Rock-Paper-Scissors with your children. (Did you know there is actually a Rock-Paper-Scissors World Championship with more than 1,000 people from around the world competing?)

4. Fill a dishpan or tub with uncooked rice or popcorn. Simply sit with your children as they play with the rice. (Obviously this is geared toward younger kids.)

5. Do a spontaneous scavenger hunt. Ask your children to bring you something red or an item that is smaller than a bagel. Make up the next clue as they race through the house, searching for the item.

6. Get a large piece of butcher paper and then trace each family member's body on the paper. Embellish

the flat bodies by drawing hair, facial features and clothes.

7. Count various items in your house. Ask kids to count the number of trees in your backyard, the number of bricks in the fireplace and how many steps lead down to the basement.

8. Put socks on your hands and sing songs together with your faceless puppets.

9. Give children a word and see what rhyming words they can come up with.

10. Give each child a piece of paper on which you've drawn a simple shape, such as a lopsided circle or a square with a dot in the middle. Ask children to draw a picture, incorporating the shape into their masterpiece.

Week Four

Do your children now think you are an amazing, fun-loving parent? Here's your chance to "relax" this week. Ask each child to plan a fun activity for the family. Offer to buy a few supplies if they need something special for their activity (anything but a new swimming pool for the backyard). Assign each child a time during the week when he or she shows creativity as the "Family Fun Master."

Have you noticed a change in your family? Has some tension disappeared? Statistics show a preschooler laughs an average of 400 times a day (those potty jokes are awfully funny). Adults? They laugh a grand total of 15 times a day. As a professional speaker, I'm frequently asked to give presentations to business groups on the importance of incorporating humor into the workplace. Study after study demonstrates that humor does three things: (1) reduces stress, (2) increases creativity, and (3) increases productivity. Major corporations pay consultants to tell them what Fun-Filled Parents have known all along: Things go better with laughter.

Children don't care whether you are a top-level executive or a house painter—children want parents who take the time to listen, to laugh and to be with them in a relaxed setting. Case in point: When my daughter Sondra was a preschooler, we often went mall walking before the stores opened. She had free reign to run the length of the mall, waving to her senior-citizen friends. One day she decided to wear her tap shoes because they made such a delightful tap-tap sound as she walked the mall's tile floors. I then met a friend who asked, "Why are you letting her wear tap shoes at the mall?" Why not? She had a great time demonstrating her shuffle-ball-change step to any person commenting on her tap shoes. Parents are all too quick to say no—and for no good reason.

Instead of thinking about schedules and methods of discipline, think about adding an element of humor and spontaneity to everyday routines. Start a pillow fight. Serve green eggs and ham for breakfast. Try to laugh more than 15 times a day. Laughter unites a group in a positive, common experience. If you've just finished a game of Hide and Seek with your children, they certainly will be more receptive to your requests for help setting the table.

A more relaxed style of parenting puts everyone in a better mood. Rather than nagging about scattered Legos, give everyone a large soup spoon. Join your children in using a spoon to race and scoop up the colorful interlocking pieces into a large pot. Fun really does make all the difference.

One morning, my daughter was calmly eating breakfast before school (as the ever-dutiful mother, I was quizzing her on her spelling words). Suddenly my husband, Allan, burst through the door and said, "Sondra, I'm on my way to a meeting, but I have

exactly five minutes to challenge you to a game of tetherball."
She raced outside, barefoot and in pajamas, for a wild game of
tetherball. What do you think had a greater impact—knowing
that there are two *Us* in the word "vacuum," or realizing that her
dad thought enough of her to stop at the house on a workday
morning just to spend a few minutes with his precious daughter?

That sense of joy and spontaneity develops into an overall
attitude of optimism about life. It's logical that the signs of a
healthy family include the ability to foster a sense of humor
among family members. One mother of three boys summed it
up like this: "If I'm going to laugh about this situation in five
years, why not just laugh about it now?"

Recently at a parenting conference, one father shared with
the group how he had made a conscious effort to create a family
atmosphere in which children enjoyed being home. He even went
so far as to make learning multiplication tables fun. He would
stand at one end of the living room while his son sat on the
couch. Dad would pose a multiplication problem, and if his son
could come up with the correct answer in two seconds, the delighted child could throw a pillow at his dad's face. Naturally, if
the answer was wrong, Dad got to throw the pillow!

We all thought that was a pretty amazing dad, until another man stood up and proudly said, "I can top that. We live
in Florida, so it's still warm in the evenings when my kids do
homework. We go outside and my wife gives them one of their
'challenge' spelling words. If they spell it correctly, they get to
throw a wet sponge at me!"

As you can imagine, both men received a well-earned round
of applause.

Remember, having fun with your children doesn't mean a
12-step plan with checklists of supplies and a cost breakdown.
Let children see that it's possible to have spontaneous fun.
When you do, rest assured that these little children will develop

into godly young adults who have a positive outlook on life—and can find humor in any situation.

And If You Still Don't Believe that Fun Makes a Difference . . .

Several years ago on the first of November, my husband, Allan, and daughter Trina took a quick trip to the drug store for Band-Aids. They arrived home dragging huge bags that certainly contained more than bandages. Trina beamed while announcing, "Mom, look what we bought! Thirty-three Halloween costumes for 10 cents each! Isn't that great?"

Naturally my question was, "What will you do with 33 Halloween costumes?"

She replied, "We're going to give them to underprivileged kids next year, of course." She and Allan then spent the next hour examining the various costumes and reveling in their bargain purchases. Every Halloween she mentions how much fun it was to load up two shopping carts with Halloween costumes. A spontaneous decision to spend $3.30 ended up creating years of positive memories.

2

Down with Dull Devotions

Do not withhold good from those to whom it is due,
when it is in your power to do it.

PROVERBS 3:27

It began as a typical conversation between two long-time friends. Maggie described her family vacation by saying, "We stayed in this great condo right on the beach on Maui. It was so convenient we really never left."

"Didn't you go snorkeling or try surfing or do some other fun stuff?" I asked.

What Maggie said next proved her eligibility for the Spiritual Mom of the Year award. "We didn't have time to do much else," she continued. "After sleeping in, we'd have a leisurely breakfast and then have devotions, which usually lasted two hours."

I gasped in shock. Do families actually have devotions while on vacation? For two hours? In our family, 15 minutes of a Bible story plus an object lesson meant we were having a spiritually charged day.

As parents, we want our children to grow up with core Christian values as a natural part of their lives. So, along with sending our kids to Sunday School and trying to live a godly life, many of us feel the need to have family devotions. Yet problems arise when we get stuck at coming up with ways to give significance to family devotions.

Which scenario fits your family? You announce, "Time for devotions!"

- Children scatter to all parts of the house to do homework. Your son actually picks up his math workbook, letting you know he can't be disturbed.

- Your spouse whispers, "Did you prepare something, or was it my turn to lead devotions?"

- Your announcement is greeted with moans of "Not again" or "But that's so boring"—or my personal favorite, "Why do we have to do this?"

- You hear the vacuum running (is that really your son pushing that thing?), and your daughter disappears to walk the dog.

- Family members quickly gather with their Bibles and display their best "church behavior" for a meaningful time of worship and study.

Most families experience "all of the above" (well, maybe all except that last item). Perhaps your plan to have family devotions started with great enthusiasm and creativity. You prepared in advance, gathering frankincense and myrrh to create the perfect object lesson. Your family ate a healthy snack as you lead a discussion about biblical principles. Children even asked appropriate questions. This amazing family devotion ended with a craft project designed to reinforce the lesson.

Fast forward a few days and soon the grandiose plans gave way to a quick, "Sit down while I read this psalm for family devotions. Then it's bedtime." Is it any wonder our children roll their eyes in dismay at the thought of family devotions?

What would a Fun-Filled Parent do in this case? Most likely, he or she would have a plan that is both practical and interactive. Children (like adults) don't respond well to a strict set of rules that tell them, "We're having devotions and you better get used to it."

Silvana's Four-Week
"Let's Get Started Having Devotions" Program

Week One

For some families, getting started is the hardest part of planning devotions. The decision to spend time together studying and praying may meet with resistance from some family members. Start out with a once-a-week meeting time. Experiment with some Bible study, related games and even crafts. See what works best for your family and then create family devotions that suit your particular needs and interests. If the once-a-week schedule is successful, add another day.

At one time or another, we've all seen an episode of *Oprah* where she stages a grandiose event like giving everyone in the audience a new car. Yet she also suggests smaller, more practical ideas to improve our lives. One of Oprah's recurring themes is encouraging people to keep an Attitude of Gratitude Journal. Why not try this in your family? Give each family member a new Attitude of Gratitude Journal. Lead the family in a casual discussion about gratitude. What does "gratitude" actually mean? Ask each family member to read a verse you've selected in advance and glue it inside the cover of his or her journal.

Bring out a stopwatch or egg timer. Have each family member spend 60 seconds listing all the things he or she is thankful for. Younger children may simply draw pictures. After the time is up, share the lists.

Spend a few minutes praying and thanking God for the numerous blessings your family has received. Encourage family members to write down their thoughts about thankfulness on a regular basis.

Close the devotion time by changing the words to the ever-popular "If You're Happy and You Know It." Try singing, "If you're thankful and you know it . . . rub your stomach," or even better, "If you're thankful and you know it . . . do a summersault."

Week Two

Begin the time together by asking family members to share what they wrote in their journals during the past week.

Ask children how they can show their gratitude. It's very easy to recite phrases such as "I'm thankful for my house" and "I'm glad we have food to eat." Explain that the family will be looking for ways to share all the good things they have.

Begin by writing letters (yes, real letters, not emails) to relatives and friends. Set out an assortment of colored paper, markers and stickers. Encourage each person in your family to make a card or write a letter. Have younger children draw pictures or decorate the envelopes. Pray for each person to whom you wrote a letter.

Week Three

For your devotions this week, begin by reading a few Bible verses on being thankful. Then go on a "thankfulness walk" around your neighborhood. As you walk, point out positive aspects of your neighborhood and express gratitude for them. For example, "I'm thankful Mrs. Johnson has such pretty flowers by her mailbox." "I'm thankful people have cars in case they need to get to a hospital quickly." For a fun twist on walking around the neighborhood, do a Heads-Tails Walk. At every corner, take turns flipping a coin. "Heads" means you turn left. If "tails" shows up, you turn right. Will you ever make it home again?

How do you feel about these family devotions so far? After this week, you'll get a smorgasbord of ideas so that you can pick and choose to see what fits in with your family's needs and personalities.

Week Four

Have the family sit at a newspaper-covered table, or outside if possible. Ahead of time, cut a few small branches from a tree. Let younger children fill a large flowerpot with dirt. Poke the sticks in the dirt. (Granted, this is not the most attractive table center-piece, but it does serve a purpose.) As a family, cut out 20 to 30 paper leaves. Don't worry if they don't look Martha Stewart per-fect. Punch a hole in one end of each leaf and tie a piece of yarn, about 6 inches long.

During the following week, whenever anyone finds some-thing to give thanks for, he or she jots it on the paper leaf and hangs it on the tree. If guests come to your house, ask them to participate also. You can make more paper leaves if you run out. Take time to occasionally stop and read what is on each leaf.

Ask the Fun Consultant

Silvana, our family needs to have devotions but I don't know where to start! How about a few ideas I can use to keep devotions interesting?

Here's an easy way to remember some principles for family devo-tions (just remember to be flexible and adjust the ideas so that they fit your family's needs and personality). Try using the B-I-B-L-E acrostic as a guideline for devotions that won't have fam-ily members hiding in the closet.

B: Be Brief

Younger children are unable to sit for 30 minutes as you read 3 chapters from the Bible. It's much easier to start with short devotions and have your children say, "Please, Mom! Let's play the Bible memory game again!" Short, to-the-point devotions give your children a positive feeling about your time together.

I: Invite Children to Participate

You are not a pastor preaching on a Sunday morning. (And if you are a pastor, relax and remember that you don't have to preach during family devotions.) Ask children to lead singing (one creative 10-year-old used her allowance to buy inexpensive kazoos for the family—she'd select a song and have the family "hum" the tune). Your two-year-old can lead everyone in "making a joyful noise unto the Lord" by clapping his hands and stomping his feet. Older children can prepare an object lesson. If you're using a book of prepared devotions, let your daughter select a lesson and present it to the rest of the family. During the devotion, ask for input. Children listen more attentively if they know they can interject or comment on the topic.

B: Bring Something to Touch, Taste or See

Children *and* adults respond to props or visuals. (Look how popular PowerPoint and Keynote presentations have become in the workplace—people in a business meeting enjoy watching the motion of color-coded pie charts. Who would have guessed?) Naturally, you'll try to incorporate the Bible in your lesson, but also find a magazine picture, an item in the house or a food item to reinforce the topic. Are you talking about manna in the desert? Serve a plain, dry cracker and ask the family how they'd like to eat nothing but that manna-like food day after day.

L: Laugh

Family devotions are a time for the family to be connected as they learn more about their Christian faith. It's okay to do that with an occasional giggle or outburst of laughter. One family started their devotions with a joke or riddle from the *Good Clean Jokes* book. Keep in mind that there's a difference between positive laughter and mean-spirited joking. If the dog decides to begin snoring during family prayer, allow the kids (and the hubby, too) to giggle and thank God for giving you a devoted family pet.

E: Evaluate from Time to Time

You may feel your devotions are filled with deep insight that is profoundly improving your family's spiritual life. Your 10-year-old may be thinking, *If I sit here quietly, Mom won't nag and we'll get done sooner and then I can go have some fun.* Ask family members to give their input about what is working and what isn't. Should you meet at a different time? What about having devotions every other day? How can the kids get more involved?

Silvana, those ideas are great, but we are so busy. I just don't have time to get my family together for devotions. We barely have time to get teeth brushed at night.

If you look at your daily schedule, you'll see that you make time to do what is important to you. Do you find time for a weekly phone chat with a friend? Do your children arrive on time for soccer or dance classes? If you think soccer is important, you'll do what you can to get them there on time. If you think family devotions are important, you'll find a way to make it happen.

Your children eat breakfast, right? So why not have devotions during breakfast? Discussing a simple devotion over a family meal is a wonderful way to start the day.

Or what about evening devotions? One creative mother of two young children gave her children baths every other night so that on alternating nights, they had family devotions in a relaxed setting. (Do your children really get so sweaty, grimy and filthy that they need a daily bath? Many Europeans still think Americans are crazy for showering every day.)

What about Saturday mornings? When did it become a law that children spend their Saturday mornings watching cartoons? Turn off the TV and enjoy quality family devotions instead of the frenzied atmosphere created by all those cartoons.

Silvana, sometimes the Bible is complicated and difficult to understand. How can I make God's Word accessible to my children?

As with most things in life, creative thinking solves many problems. Instead of throwing up your hands in despair and proclaiming, "I'm raising heathens because we don't have devotions!" just relax. You can easily find family devotion books that have everything written out so that you just follow the step-by-step directions. Who needs to be creative when someone else has done all the work and put it in an easy-to-read format?

One mom simply got an old Sunday School lesson book from the back of the church storage closet. She would glance at a lesson plan and pick and choose which activities applied to her family.

Some churches have suggestions for family devotions listed on their websites. You might get a wealth of ideas by signing up for their daily online devotional.

Another idea is to keep reading and get some suggestions to help make family devotions burst with creative activities. Here comes the creativity! The drama! The biblical principles! Here come the ideas for amazing family devotions!

The following are ideas for family devotions that run the gamut from serious to silly to thought-provoking. Look over the suggestions and see what works best for your family. The whole point of family devotions is to experience God's greatness by sharing, praying and bonding together as a family.

- Read the story of Zacchaeus and discuss the change Jesus brought into his life. Have your kids ever climbed a tree? Get brave and go tree climbing. Don't forget to sing the song "Zacchaeus was a wee little man . . ."

- Jonah spent three days inside a big fish (talk about fish breath!). Re-create the hot, crowded conditions inside the fish. Put a large blanket over a table. Have the family sit under the table while reading the story about Jonah. Is it getting uncomfortable? Would you want to stay there for three days?

- Matthew 5:13 says we are the salt of the earth. Have your family taste several varieties of salt—sea salt, table salt and seasoning salt. Now eat some potatoes without salt, and then try them with each different kind of salt. Which type adds the most flavor? What does it mean when Jesus tells us that we are the salt of the earth?

- Collect all the Bibles in your house. If you are like many families, you have everything from colorful picture Bibles to the *King James Version*. Pick a verse and read it from different versions. Which version is best suited for the entire family to use during devotion time?

- Jesus humbled Himself by washing the disciples' feet. If you have older children, wash their feet as a sign of your love for them.

- Get wild! Children always hear the story of David and Goliath. Get a real slingshot and let children see what it's like to shoot a rock at a tree. This is one family devotion time your kids won't forget!

- Bring out all the stuffed animals and pretend they are lions. Put them in a "pit" and act out the story of Daniel in the lion's den. Younger children are responsible for creating ferocious lion roars.

- The battle of Jericho got pretty loud. Build a tower from boxes, blocks or pillows. March around your Jericho, hooting and hollering. Do the walls come tumbling down?

- Next time you see a wig at a garage sale, spend 50 cents and buy it. Act out the story of Samson and Delilah. One child, wearing a wig, shows his strength by flexing his muscles and lifting his younger sister. "Delilah" comes along and cuts some of his hair. Horror! His strength is gone! Have the children take turns wearing the wig.

And If You Still Don't Believe that Fun Makes a Difference . . .

As with most families, we aren't that consistent with having devotions. One week, Allan decided to make up for our lack of family devotions by *really* making a Bible story come alive for his Sunday School class. He dragged a canoe into the church, down the hall and into the cramped kindergarten Sunday School room. When it was time for the story about Jesus sleeping in the boat during the giant storm, he had the class sit inside the canoe and pretend to be the disciples. I read the story as he rocked the "boat." The young kids shouted, "Jesus, wake up! We're in a big storm!" Parents started to arrive just as we finished the lesson. Imagine their surprise to see children rocking back and forth in a canoe, yelling for Jesus to wake up and getting sprayed with warm water from a spray bottle (c'mon, we had to have some real sea spray!).

3

Taming Television Time

Television has changed the American child from an
irresistible force to an immoveable object.
LAURENCE J. PETER

Pretend you invited a guest to visit your home. Every morning as you served breakfast to your children, he talked in the background, suggesting you serve "All New Super Crunchy, Super Sweet Breakfast Sugar Bombs." Then your guest said things like, "Get a grip, dude," when you asked children to brush their teeth. After school, your guest showed your children how to bonk their brother on the head with a frying pan. Then he suggested they talk back to their parents and lie about having finished their homework. Throughout the evening, your guest displayed rude behavior, including burping at the dinner table. Right before bed, your guest demonstrated what it's like to shoot someone.

Would you invite that guest to return? Probably not.

Many people call television the "uninvited guest" in their homes.

Children exposed to violence and inappropriate behavior on TV are likely to imitate what they see. That's why a parent—yes, an ordinary parent—needs to step in and restrict TV use. There are numerous ways for parents to control the "uninvited guest" in their home.

As you consider ways to improve the TV-viewing habits of members of your household, answer these questions:

1. If your children wanted to only eat Twinkies and marshmallows at every meal, would you allow it?

2. If your children refused to wear seatbelts in the car, would you let them ride anyway?

3. If your children wanted to bring a radio into the bathtub, would you let them?

Like most parents, you answered an emphatic "no" to all of the above. We know eating junk food—not to mention combining electricity and water—isn't good for our children. We know, too, that too much television viewing isn't either. Consider the following sobering statistics from the TV Turn-off Network:

- 40 percent of families always or often have the TV on during dinner.
- The TV is on a daily average of 7 hours, 40 minutes in the American home.
- 48 percent of children have a television in their bedroom.
- By the time the average child is 18, he or she will have watched 200,000 acts of violence and 16,000 murders on TV.
- 91 percent of children say they feel "scared" or "worried" by violent scenes on TV.
- Parents spend an average of 38.5 minutes a week in meaningful conversation with their children.[1]

So what can a Fun-Filled Parent do to curtail TV watching? Come up with a concrete plan to help your child fill her time in a creative, productive way.

Silvana's Four-Week
"Let's Get Started Cutting TV Time" Program

Week One

Plan a family meeting so that everyone feels he or she has input in the situation. Begin by stating that as the parent, you know the family needs to cut back on screen time: TV *and* video games. Brainstorm a list of ways to make this possible. Explain that this is a four-week "experiment"—as a family, you're going to cut back on TV time in order to do other fun things.

Don't expect your children to smile and say, "Thanks, Mom and Dad. Watching less TV gives me more time to concentrate on my homework, which results in getting into an Ivy League college so that I can get a good job and buy you both a new house." Begin by making a few minor adjustments. If the TV is on during dinner, turn it off. If children watch three shows after school, try allowing them only two shows. Making subtle changes to TV-viewing habits shows children that life can go on without a TV constantly blaring in the background.

Week Two

Ask your children how they felt about the small changes. Do they still feel deprived? This week, bring out the weekly TV schedule and have family members pick two or three shows they want to watch. Write these down. Instead of randomly watching whatever is on TV, the kids can only turn the TV on when it's time for their approved show. When the show ends, the TV goes off.

Week Three

Brainstorm with your children a list of things to do besides watching TV. Yes, they'll include things like "Take a trip to Disneyland" and "Build a swimming pool in the backyard." That's fine—let them dream. Along with those creative ideas, you'll also end up with a list that includes ideas like playing with the dog and working on a puzzle.

The goal this week is for your family to cut their TV-viewing time in half. When children claim they'll die of boredom, simply point to the list. They'll soon find ways to creatively fill their time. They may even read a book! Simply remember, the boredom will pass.

Week Four

This is the tough week—it's TV-free week. Yes, turn the TV off for the entire week. Some families find that by this time they don't even miss watching TV.

When you begin the traumatic experience of eliminating your family's TV time, help children with the transition. Buy a few new games or craft supplies. It's unfair to say "No TV" without giving children an alternative. In a few weeks, they will surprise you by coming up with their own ideas. In the beginning though, provide a few activities. Give each child $5 and then hit the garage sales—they'll be able to buy inexpensive "new" books, dress-up clothes or games to use.

One dad, knowing his children were upset about his eliminating their TV time, planned a short activity each evening. "Sometimes I'd sit at work, frantic because I hadn't

How to Throw a Spark Party

Step 1
Buy a package of Wintergreen Life Savers.

Step 2
Take a child in a dark closet.

Step 3
Place Life Savers between front teeth and . . . *bite!*

Step 4
Laugh at how bright sparks fly out of your mouth.

Step 5
Repeat for extra fun.

Step 6
Leave closet.

Step 7
End of party!

come up with anything fun to do that night," he shared. His children relished the extra fun time with dad, even if it simply meant a game of Hide and Seek, Sumo wrestling with pillows stuffed under their shirts, or a Spark Party.

Ask the Fun Consultant

Silvana, I know my children watch too much TV. When I yell and turn it off, they start bickering with each other, which drives me crazy. So I turn the TV back on just to have peace. What are some ways to get them involved in other activities?

Your children are very smart! They've already learned what it takes to break your resolve to limit their TV-viewing time. With a little effort (and the ability to ignore their bickering), you can cut back on their TV time while also getting them involved in worthwhile activities.

- After going through the "Let's Get Started" program, explain that watching TV is a privilege, not a right. Children should ask before turning on the set. One mom had a rule that the TV could go on if the rec room was clean. That meant all toys and food items were gone, pillows placed on the couch, and the floor cleared of any debris. She was amazed at how often her children got involved in other activities just so that they wouldn't have to clean up the TV room. In that situation, you are not denying children TV. You're actually saying, "Yes! By all means watch TV . . . after the TV room is clean. Enjoy your show."

- Try not to use TV as a reward. When you say, "If you eat your beans, you'll get chocolate cake for dessert," it makes children crave chocolate cake. In the same way, rewarding good grades or polite behavior with the promise of extra TV time creates the false impression that watching TV is something special—something that they should desire.

- If limiting TV time on a daily basis is difficult, try eliminating it entirely on certain days. That way, children know they can watch their (approved) shows on Monday, Wednesday and Friday. On Tuesday and Thursdays, the TV remains off. One family decided the family could watch a reasonable amount of TV on weeknights, but on the weekends, the TV stayed off, allowing more time for family interaction. See what works best for your family.

- Is the television set the focal point of your home? How about moving it to a location that isn't so accessible? One clever mother told her children that they could continue to watch as much TV as they wanted. There was only one difference. She actually replaced the large color TV with an "antique" black-and-white set, which she set up in the storage area of the basement. If children wanted to watch TV, they could sit among the boxes of dusty Christmas decorations and squint at the tiny screen.

Silvana, now that we're watching less TV, do you have ideas for how to turn our TV time into meaningful family time so that we don't just stare at the screen and "vegetate"?

It's obvious that TV viewing is an emotional, hot-button issue for parents, too. So often we use TV as a way of dealing with the

day-to-day stress of modern life—and of raising kids. How often
do we suggest to our kids, "Why don't you watch TV while I . . . "?
How often do we cheat them out of quality time with us—and
with each other?

And it's too easy to substitute "educational and spiritual
videos" for TV programming. The point is still the same: Children passively sit in front of a screen. (We're probably the only
Christian family in the world that has never owned a *Veggie Tales*
video.) Save the videos for when a child is sick or when you're
stuck in a vacation cabin with 10 straight days of rain.

Instead of seeing TV as a babysitter for children, use it as a
tool for learning and interactive family time:

- One family had a rule that family members had to do
  jumping jacks or run in place during commercials!
  This certainly gave the children an awareness of how
  many commercials filled their viewing time. It also
  broke up the monotony of mindlessly sitting in front
  of the screen.

- Sit next to your child to discuss the program. Talk
  about the characters. Ask questions such as "Why do
  you think that boy is so mean to his little brother?"
  "That boy kicked his dog because he was mad. What
  should you do if you get mad?" "This show makes it
  look like girls can't do math. What do you think
  about that?"

- Elaborate on television programs. If your family en-
  joys Shark Week on the Discovery channel, get some
  library books on sharks. Visit an aquarium to see
  sharks close up. Make a papier mâché shark as a table
  centerpiece. This way TV is simply a supplement to
  educating and entertaining your family.

Our family loves Broadway musicals. My daughter knew the entire scores of *Phantom of the Opera* and *Les Miserables* by the time she was four. (Yes, I know it's not the most age-appropriate material, but she also knew the score to *Joseph and the Amazing Technicolor Dreamcoat*.) Each year, we look forward to watching the Tony Awards on TV, highlighting all the Broadway shows we love. When Sondra was nine, she and my husband spent three hours preparing for the Tony Awards show.

Since we couldn't be in New York to see the Tonys, Allan and Sondra brought New York to our family room. They began by drawing the entire New York skyline on a 12-foot length of butcher paper, which was then hung on one wall. They dug out Christmas lights and filled the room with lights to rival Times Square. And since no Tony Awards show is complete without the red carpet, Allan and Sondra taped red construction paper down the entire hall (we're very low budget). They prepared some fancy finger foods and poured sparkling cider in elegant plastic glasses. Then we all dressed up in our fanciest clothes, walked the red carpet and sat among the lights of New York, watching the Tony Awards . . . all in the comfort of our home.

If cutting back on TV time still seems too difficult, then wait until the third week in April, which is National TV Turnoff Week. Tell your family it's time to celebrate. This might be a great time to kick off the plan to limit your family's TV viewing. One second-grader, after participating in TV Turnoff Week, said, "I had a great time and my only question is: If this is so great, why don't we turn off the TV the rest of the year?" Check out their website for startling facts about the negative effects of TV on children: www.tvturnoff.org.

Some of you are thinking, *This is sooooooo hard! I know my children watch too much TV, but I don't think we can make the change.* But let me tell you from personal experience: Even the most

TV-addicted family can make the positive change to reduce the amount of TV watched in their home.

Our family had a very unique experience when we were asked to appear on the Fox reality show *Trading Spouses*. (Yes, even though we hardly watch TV, we ended up appearing on TV.) For this show, I spent a week living with a family in another state while their mom stayed with Allan and Sondra. Even though I didn't know the ages of the children, I packed an assortment of craft supplies such as fabric crayons, wooden racecars to decorate, cardboard dinosaurs and a kaleidoscope kit. I also brought books and even a parachute for group games.

Upon arriving at the new home, I discovered that the 3 children, ages 8, 12 and 17, spent their summer days watching R-rated TV and videos for 14 to 16 hours a day. Breakfast consisted of coffee. Around noon, the kids complained about headaches. Lunch consisted of ice cream eaten directly from the carton while watching more TV.

Trading Spouses is designed so that for the first two days I fit into their lifestyle, which meant sitting on the couch watching TV (this was the hardest part of the entire experience). On the third day I declare, "Now we'll do things *my* way." Of course, the first change I made was to turn off the TV. Horrors! The 12-year-old boy put on his football helmet, stuck his thumb in his mouth and dramatically rocked his head against the wall, saying, "I can't live without TV. I can't live without TV!" He miraculously survived. Instead of watching TV, we went hiking and rode bikes. I sent the shell-shocked dad off with his kids to go bowling and visit a museum. He was used to sitting in his leather recliner watching TV while working from home.

Then the crafts appeared. We started with the kaleidoscope kit. The very macho dad made constant negative comments, including four letter words that weren't "glue" and "lace." He called his 12-year-old son a "sissy" for enjoying the craft project.

Still, I was making progress, because throughout the next four days, the two younger kids kept asking if I had more crafts. We created a shelf where they could display their creations for their mom, and asked the TV crew to bring more supplies because the family didn't even have colored markers or construction paper. The most beautiful moment was when the so-called hyperactive eight-year-old spent two hours intensely mixing paint colors together—she'd never used paints before and was fascinated that red and white paint created pink.

Then when their friends came over, I brought out the parachute, and we played games together. No one complained of being bored.

On the day I left, the dad sheepishly said, "I actually had fun doing some of those crazy things you had us do." (Of course, he could have simply been saying that out of relief that I was leaving his house.) The kids had flourished. They had had time to read and draw detailed pictures. The eight-year-old had learned the joys of playing dress-up, as she dressed in whimsical clothes, and we designed a matching whimsical hairstyle, complete with a toilet roll and numerous multicolored ribbons.

Beautiful things happened when this family went cold-turkey on their addiction to the TV. It was a unique situation, yet it shows that it's possible to get kids engaged in creative activities—even kids used to watching TV for 14 to 16 hours a day. (I'm sure they turned the TV on the minute I left the house, but both parents did tell me they were going to make a serious attempt to cut back on TV time.)

If that family could survive a week without TV, then your family can certainly survive cutting back the amount of time you watch.

Need some ideas to fill in your extra time? Simply visit any bookstore. You'll find hundreds of books filled with easy-to-do activities. Or, hey—how about continuing to read this book?

You will find ideas guaranteed to bring your family some fun and laughter . . . without that obnoxious uninvited guest, the TV set.

And If You Still Don't Believe that Fun Makes a Difference . . .

It's easy for kids to believe all the grandiose claims made by commercials—which is why it's so important to teach our kids not to take them seriously. In our family we often play a "ridicule the commercial" game while watching TV: As soon as a commercial comes on, we mute the sound and make up our own words to the commercial. Our new voice-overs say something like, "Yes, if you take this nail fungus medicine, you too will have cute bugs crawling under your toenails. In fact, the bugs may crawl all over your body! Wouldn't it be great to go on a picnic with your family and share the bugs with family and friends?"

Try playing this game with your family. Commercials will never be the same! And you might just find that your kids don't believe everything they see on TV.

Note
1. "Fact Sheet" from the Center for Screen Time Awareness. http://www.screentime.org/facts.php?id=35 (accessed February 2008).

4

Family Fitness for Nonfitness Fanatics

There's no easy way out [of exercising]. If there were, I would have bought it. And believe me, it would be one of my favorite things!

OPRAH WINFREY[1]

On a trip to Holland, my husband and I were strolling through a neighborhood at dusk in a tiny town called Giethorn. As it got darker, I began to feel like a Peeping Tom—none of the people had closed their curtains or window shades. We "peeked" into each home, catching glimpses of Dutch family life. One window revealed a family laughing at the dinner table. Through another window we saw an elderly couple reading the paper, a contented cat on each lap. Later, our Bed and Breakfast owner explained that the Dutch feel they have nothing to hide, so there's no need to close the curtains.

If people taking a walk passed by your home and peeked inside, what would they see? A family of couch potatoes? Kids eating sugary snacks while playing video games? In that case, here are some ideas how to get your family off the couch.

Did you panic just now at the thought of getting your family started on a physical fitness program? Don't worry—this doesn't mean you have to turn into a drill sergeant. Fitness doesn't involve a 10-mile run before breakfast while drinking a dozen raw eggs. No, it simply means finding structured and unstructured ways to get you and your family walking, skipping, jumping, dribbling, riding, jogging and dancing (not all at the same time of course). Being a Fun-Filled Parent gives you the opportunity to incorporate fitness in ways a drill sergeant would never attempt. So get a calendar and declare the next four weeks your family's chance to make some changes that eventually will lead to better health and increased family physical fitness.

Silvana's Four-Week "Let's Get Started Being Fit" Program

Week One
- *Tuesday and Thursday*: Eat fresh fruit for dessert.
- *Friday*: Take the family swimming or for a bike ride.

Was that so hard?

Week Two
- *Tuesday, Wednesday, Thursday*: Drink water for dinner instead of sugary drinks. At mealtimes, serve slightly smaller portions than usual.
- *Saturday*: Check with the local Parks and Recreation Department or nature center to see if they offer family hikes. Then participate in the activity.

See? You're surviving!

Week Three
- *Monday through Thursday*: Serve whole-grain cereal for breakfast, topped with two tablespoons of normal sugary cereal. If your children take the bus to school, leave your house a few minutes early and walk to the stop after the one they usually take.
- *Saturday*: Make individual homemade vegetable pizzas using prepared pizza dough. Let family members top their

pizza with an assortment of low-fat cheeses and broccoli, mushrooms, zucchini, onions, and so on.

- *Sunday*: Have a picnic in the park after church. Fly a kite or toss Frisbees back and forth.

Week Four

Look at the changes you've made during the last three weeks. Those gradual changes are beginning to add up to better fitness and health for your family. For the last week on this program, see if your library has some older fitness videos. Your kids will get a kick out of seeing Jane Fonda or Richard Simmons lead exercises. Try to work out together with the videos at least three times this week. Then plan a secret outing that involves fitness. Leave clues such as "Be ready to leave the house by 10:00 A.M. Saturday" and "You'll have a chance to lift something very heavy." Then take the family bowling or to play tennis on a community court. There's nothing like a surprise adventure to make physical fitness enjoyable.

Congratulations! You've just completed your first physical-fitness training program (and it was so much cheaper than going to the gym). Just making a few changes allows your family to become more active and eat healthier. And I bet they've even enjoyed the process.

Ask the Fun Consultant

I know our whole family needs to exercise more. How can we change our tried-and-true habits? It's so easy to plop down on the couch, watch a video and call it "quality family time." Any suggestions?

Any type of change is hard to make—it doesn't matter in what area of your life that change has to be made. The idea is to start with small, gradual changes that eventually lead up to a family that runs triathlons, eats alfalfa sprout sandwiches and leaps tall buildings in a single bound!

How about trying some of these simple ideas?

- When you're out shopping, park at the far end of the parking lot. You're less likely to get your car dinged by a careless driver and your family gets exercise. How's that for a 2-for-1 special?

- Try taking a pre-bedtime walk around your neighborhood. (Maybe some people will have their curtains open, like the Dutch.) One family with three preschoolers had an evening ritual of dinner, walk, bath, story, bed. If it rained, the family simply took umbrellas. During the winter, they continued their walks even in the dark and cold.

- Check local Parks and Recreation departments for events such as open gyms or free hikes. Many communities offer "All-Comers Track Meets." Families just show up and participate in various track-and-field events. Dad can show off his prowess throwing the shot put, and Junior can jump the hurdles. Sondra still has the first-place ribbon she won as a 3-year-old in the 100-meter dash. I think she won even while stopping halfway to look at a caterpillar crossing the track.

- Next time relatives come over, divide the clan into several groups of 3 to 4 people. Then have each group go to a different part of the house and practice some exercise routines like you'd see on TV. Appoint someone to videotape these routines, complete with background music. Costumes add a very professional touch. Get Grandpa to wear a sweatband around his head and a muscle shirt while leading an exercise routine to a polka music beat. After each group has recorded its routine, play all the routines back for the whole family. The entire group will enjoy exercising along to these one-of-a-kind routines. Even a two-year-old can lead everyone in jumping up and down. Watch out, Jane Fonda!

- Look up www.volksmarch.org to find a local Volksmarch group. You're probably asking, "What is a Volksmarch?" Volksmarchers are happy hikers who have clubs around the world. They actually don't "march"; they walk. They set up designated courses in various communities, and you simply follow the signs to complete the route. Children like being leaders and following the designated trail markers. The atmosphere is very festive as people walk, push strollers and lead dogs along the route.

- Speaking of dogs, a great way to exercise is to find your dog's leash and take good old Rover for a muchneeded walk. No dog? Borrow a neighbor's.

- Contact your local YMCA to see if they are participating in the Activate America program, co-sponsored by Kimberly-Clark. This nationwide program encourages families to play together while getting exercise.[2]

These ideas should get you started on your way to family fitness. But some of you probably have another question. Go ahead—ask.

Silvana, I'll try to get my family to move more. But here's the biggest problem: How can I convince my family to eat fruits and vegetables

instead of chips, candy, ice cream, cake, donuts, sugared drinks,
Cheetos and the occasional deep-fried Twinkie?

Americans do love their snacks. Yet I have to ask: How do young children get those high-calorie, high-fatty foods? This sounds simplistic, but if adults don't bring junk food into the house, it's unlikely that a six-year-old will walk to the store and use his allowance to buy a candy bar. So, unless Willy Wonka is sponsoring another contest and you need to find the Golden Ticket, begin by cutting down on the snacks you buy. You'll get some complaints, but if children are hungry enough, they'll soon learn to enjoy dried banana chips or fruit-juice popsicles.

Try the S.N.A.C.K. approach as you help your family modify their poor eating habits.

S: Send Children Shopping

Don't worry. This doesn't mean you let your 10-year-old twins loose in the grocery store with a shopping cart and your checkbook. Do some research about healthy foods. With the family, make an extensive list, writing down foods that are low in sugar and fat. Next time you shop with your children, have them select some foods from the list. This gives children power to make choices. Each choice is already parent-approved, so there's no arguing involved. If your daughter selects raspberry juice bars, she'll be inclined to eat them at snack time.

Remember when I suggested you research healthy foods? Surprise! Here's a partial list to get you going.

- Any type of cut-up fruit or vegetables
- Applesauce cups
- Baked chips in small quantities
- Frozen fruit bars
- Fruit kabobs

- Jicama
- Light popcorn
- Low-fat granola
- Low-fat granola bars
- Low-fat yogurt
- Low-fat cheese
- Pretzels
- Pumpkin seeds
- Raisins or dried fruit
- Rice cakes
- Tortillas with low-fat cheese
- Whole-grain fig bars

N: No More Sugary Soft Drinks and Juice Packs

Water and milk are still the best choices when it comes to liquid nourishment. Make an ordinary glass of water special by
adding a few ice cubes made from pure juice. The colorful orange or grape juice ice cubes add a festive look to the water.
When packing lunches, add 100-percent juice packs rather than
"fruit-flavored drinks." As far as soda goes, it's obvious children
don't need it.

A: Avoid Mindless Snacking

It's all too easy to calm a fussy toddler with some Cheerios or
crackers. We often automatically hand our children a snack as
soon as they get in the car. Since when did riding in a car and
eating go hand in hand? In fact, most British and Europeans
can't imagine eating in cars. BMW doesn't even feature cup
holders in their cars sold in Germany.

Here's one of the hardest questions you'll find in this book.
Do you find yourself buying a latte while driving to school, going shopping or on the way to work? If Europeans want coffee
or a special cup of tea, they take the time to sit down and enjoy

Here's a visual way to estimate serving sizes

A rounded handful = about one-half cup cooked or raw veggies or cut fruit, a piece of fruit, or one-half cup of cooked rice or pasta—this is also a good measure for a snack serving such as chips or pretzels

Deck of cards = a serving of meat, fish or poultry that fits in the palm of your hand (don't count your fingers!). For example, one chicken breast, one-quarter pound hamburger patty or a medium pork chop.

Golf ball or large egg = one-quarter cup of dried fruit or nuts

Tennis ball = about one-half cup of ice cream

Computer mouse = about the size of a small baked potato

(Continued on next page)

the drinking experience. Americans, on the other hand, have become conditioned to having a high-calorie "gourmet" coffee or iced drink in their hands on a continual basis (a Vanilla Crème Frappuccino has 870 calories). Usually parents buy their children a gourmet sweetened milk or hot chocolate drink as well. There is nothing wrong with an occasional treat—just make it "special" rather than a must-have on a daily basis. Those 870 calories add up!

C: Control Portions

No more fast-food "super-sized" meals. One of the easiest ways to control weight is simply by reducing the size of portions. One mother replaced dinner-sized plates with large salad plates. She served smaller portions, but everyone still received a full plate of food. If children are still hungry after eating their meal, offer additional fruits and vegetables. And remember, in the end, smaller portions mean children don't feel deprived of their favorite foods.

K: Keep Trying!

Adapting to a new type of eating pattern is hard. Make small changes. Serve baked potato chips instead of deep-fried chips. Order from the "Healthy Menu" when eating at fast-food restaurants. Those small changes, over time, will really add up.

> Compact disc = about the size of one serving of pancake or small waffle
>
> Thumb tip = about one teaspoon of peanut butter
>
> Six dice = a serving of cheese

S: Sample New Foods

Keep interesting foods in your pantry. How about serving fortune cookies as a snack, or couscous instead of pasta? Make mealtime fun by sampling new foods beyond grilled cheese sandwiches.

Grocery stores offer a variety of exotic foods such as star fruit and purple potatoes. Go crazy in the fresh fruit section—purchase a whole pineapple and cut it up as part of a family activity. After you've mastered that, move on to cutting open a coconut. Now that's a challenge!

Now that you have some tips on improving your diet, let's get back to some thoughts on physical fitness.

Okay, Silvana: You've inspired me to get my family moving and to eat a healthier diet. But we're on a limited budget. We can't afford fancy health club membership or a ski trip to Switzerland.

Money doesn't have to be a factor in family fitness. When you were a child, did your parents sign you up for strength training at a gym? No. They probably encouraged you to play outside with friends, ride bikes and climb an occasional tree. See if any of these free or low-cost ideas can help turn your family into lean, mean, exercising machines. Above all, have fun!

- How about setting up an obstacle course? Work together collecting lawn furniture, cushions, buckets, and other odds and ends. Your course might begin in the backyard with sliding down the playground slide. Then crawling under the picnic table, running around the rose bushes, jumping over the dog house (unless you have a St. Bernard), weaving back and forth between some empty flowerpots, and ending up back at the slide. Instead of competing with each other, family members should each record his or her own individual time and then see if he or she can beat it.

- Spice up traditional board games like Monopoly and Candy Land. If you land in jail, do 10 push-ups. When you land on a yellow square, jump in place 10 times. If playing a game with dice, give each number a fitness designation. For example, roll "1," do 1 somersault. Roll "2," do 2 jumping jacks. And, well—you get the idea.

- Divide your family in half (not literally!). When you say "Go," one group walks around the house going to the left. The other half heads right. As you pass each other, make silly faces and noises, trying to make each other laugh. Walk around the house 10 to 15 times (this routine is great for exercise and giggles).

- Make Sunday morning extra special by parking a few blocks from church and walking the extra distance. One family decided to ride their bikes the three miles to church. There's less traffic on Sunday mornings, an extra incentive for riding. Just pack some deodorant and watch out for helmet hair.

- Buy an assortment of jump ropes and get a workout by skipping rope. Try doing Double Dutch. Don't forget the Red Hot Peppers!

If your school sees fitness as a low priority, make it a high priority at home. A basketball hoop provides hours of fun, especially if Mom or Dad is trying to beat Junior at a game of HORSE. Garage sales often have sports equipment that you can buy at unbeatable prices (so, no more excuses).

As an extra incentive to get kids to exercise, offer a fitness activity in place of a chore. Say something like, "Jason and Eric, I know tonight's your turn to clear the table and do the dishes. But it's such a nice evening; let's go for a bike ride instead. I'll clean the kitchen when we get back." That's an offer they surely won't turn down.

And If You Still Don't Believe that Fun Makes a Difference . . .

Fun-Filled Parents can find ways to make fitness fun. When Sondra was little, she and Allan would play "trained dolphin" in the water at our local community pool. One would be the dolphin trainer, giving commands such as "Flipper! Jump in the air and do a back flip!" The person selected to be the dolphin had to follow the commands by majestically rising out of the water and doing a back flip. Other commands might be "Swim three laps back and forth, Flipper!" Then they'd switch roles. Instead of aimlessly splashing in the water, they both had great workouts and enjoyed father-daughter fun.

Notes

1. Oprah Winfrey, *O* magazine, February 2005. http://www.quotationspage.com/subjects/exercise/ (accessed March 2008).
2. Find out more about Activate America at www.ymca.net/activateamerica.

5

Avoiding Discipline Disasters

Any child can tell you the sole purpose of a middle name is so
he can tell when he's really in trouble.

DENNIS FAKES

Warning! Warning! Disclaimer!

Here's the truth: This chapter doesn't have cute ideas about decorating birthday hats or building an obstacle course in your backyard. It's about the important but not-so-exciting topic of . . . discipline.

Hopefully you've already picked up a few Fun-Filled Parent tips to help you develop a great relationship with your kids. You've probably also noticed how discipline problems decrease as time spent with your children increases. Yet, occasionally, just every so often, you may find yourself sending a quick email to a close friend that says, "Help! Jacob is out of control. He talks back, won't do what I tell him and picks on his little sister. All I do is yell, which doesn't seem to do any good."

Your friend—and all other parents—sympathize. At shopping malls everywhere, we've seen ordinary children suddenly turn into whirling dervishes when Mom won't buy them the latest video game.

Several years ago, Allan and I visited a family with three children. It seemed like a typical home with a few toys on the floor, comfortable furniture and a refrigerator covered with notes and photographs. After the usual light-hearted conversation, the mother called her children to dinner. Seven-year-old

Steven answered, "I'll be right there, Mom. I'm just finishing this Lego model." Obviously, this reply did not suit Steven's mother. She strode into his room and we could hear her say, "Steven! When I call you, I expect you to come. I demand instant obedience!" Steven dejectedly came to the dinner table, obedient but certainly not in a positive mood.

Do we really need instant obedience from our children? Of course rules and obedience are important, but there are ways to achieve the end result without shouting or demanding instant obedience. Remember that "discipline" means "to teach." Let's look at some techniques for teaching children in a positive, loving way.

Silvana's Four-Week "Let's Get Started with Discipline" Program

Week One

Use this week to come up with four easy-to-remember household rules. Select rules that work for your family without worrying about "traditional rules." One family had a rule of "Eat only in the kitchen," while their friends next door happily let their kids eat throughout the house. Sit down together and brainstorm possible rules. Find what works best for your family. Then narrow down the rules to the four most important ones. Post copies of these rules throughout the house.

Week Two

Review the four rules you selected and decide how to enforce them. Ask your children, "We decided as a family that in our house we don't call each other names. That's a good rule. What should we do when someone breaks that rule?" Let children come up with appropriate consequences. That way, when Sara calls her brother a "gross, banana-nose jerk," you can calmly say,

"Sara, our family decided that the punishment for calling someone names is to scrub out the bottom of the outside garbage can and then apologize to the person. You'll find rags under the sink to help you get started cleaning the grime from the garbage can. Once you're finished, you can apologize to your brother."

Week Three

Make an effort to avoid saying "Okay?" when asking children to do something. If your boss said, "Please finish that report by tomorrow, okay?" you'd probably wonder if she's really asking you a question. Is she asking if it's possible to have the report done by tomorrow? What does "okay" really mean? In the same way, when you tell children "Please get ready for bed, okay?" they think an option has been implied—that it's not *really* time for bed. After all, you're asking them a question, aren't you?

Make clear statements such as, "When the timer goes off, it's time to brush your teeth and put on pajamas." That's it. You've used a statement, not a question that uses the "okay" construction.

Okay?

Week Four

This week, try to make your expectations clear to your children. Children are very literal. When setting rules for children, be very clear. Telling your son "Clean your room" is too vague. Your standard of "clean" and his are quite different. It's better to say (and write down) something like:

> **A clean room means:**
> - Bed is made
> - Dirty clothes are in hamper
> - Shoes are in closet
> - Clothes are on hangers or folded in drawers

Many times children simply don't understand what is expected. Have you ever asked a 12-year-old to show you how to do something on the computer? They whip through shortcuts and all sorts of techniques that leave you breathless. Then your daughter says, "Mom, why can't you understand how to import this file? I just showed you."

You know what you mean by "Please be on your best behavior during the plane trip." What does that mean to a six-year-old? One dad, before taking his daughter on her first plane ride, set up chairs to represent airplane seats. They role-played how not to kick seats or "accidentally" push the flight attendant call button, among other things. His daughter had a clear idea what behavior was expected, resulting in less need for discipline.

Congratulations! You've just completed the Four-Week "Let's Get Started with Discipline" program. There's always room for questions, so here goes.

Ask the Fun Consultant

Silvana, why can't my nine-year-old daughter complete basic chores? I tell her to clean the kitchen and she acts like I'm telling her to clean an Army mess hall.

Sometimes we assume that children know how to do something when in fact they really don't. When assigning your children a task such as vacuuming the car or folding laundry, try these steps:

1. Do the job while they watch. Explain the steps.
2. Have them help you with the job.
3. Let your children complete the task while you watch.
4. Get out of the way and let your child do the task alone.

Teaching self-reliance gives children a feeling of control. Watching their faces as they master a new task will make the hard work pay off. Help children to be successful in one task before encouraging them to try something else. When your child knows how to put away clean clothes, then it's time to gradually move on to other chores.

We've all heard that "Success breeds success," so let's help children make successful decisions and learn about natural consequences. For instance:

- Let toddlers decide between juice and milk.

- Let middle schoolers plan a week's worth of dinner menus (within your guidelines).

- Give kids the choice between vacuuming the car or raking leaves.

- Allow kids to decide whether they want to sign up for soccer or swim lessons.

So often, parents get hung up on little issues that cause conflict in the home. If your child doesn't like sauce on his fish, serve plain fish. There's no need to cook an extra meal, but slight variations are fine. This gives children the sense that they have some control over their lives.

One mother had trouble getting her son to eat typical breakfast foods. No matter what she tried, he didn't like toast, pancakes, waffles or eggs. He wanted chicken soup with pastina. She finally agreed and he ate his soup and pasta every morning.

Even as an adult, Tommy continued to have chicken soup and pastina often for breakfast. Tommy later became Tom Lagana, coauthor of the books *Chicken Soup for the Volunteer's Soul* and *Chicken Soup for the Prisoner's Soul*. See what can happen if you allow children to make choices?

By simply allowing children to make choices, many power struggles are avoided. When Sondra was a preschooler, we taught her the words "negotiable" and "non-negotiable." Sitting in her car seat was non-negotiable. Eating fruit for breakfast was negotiable. She learned early on that when we said, "Sondra, this is non-negotiable. You need to stay in the shallow end of the pool," we were firm in our decision. As she got older she'd say, "I want to pierce my ears. Is that a negotiable issue?"

As children gain experience in making decisions, they learn about natural consequences. Believe me, natural consequences are much more effective than Mom or Dad giving Lecture #123 on *The Virtues of a Tidy Room*. Instead of nagging, let natural consequences take place. Let me illustrate:

- Jennifer's soccer shirt is filthy because she forgot to put it in the hamper. Guess she'll have to wash it herself or wear it dirty.

- If Junior hasn't done his job of turning on the dishwasher, sit down at the dinner table and calmly say, "Junior, all the silverware is dirty. What should we do?" The key is to be a calm, collected adult.

- You may be seething that Amber didn't clean out the car on Friday afternoon, which is one of her assigned chores. But smile sweetly and say, "I certainly can't drive you to the mall in a dirty car, Amber. Let me know when you've completed your chore of vacuuming the car so I can drive you."

Silvana, you have some good ideas about discipline. But how do I communicate with my kids? Seems like I'm either yelling or they're making faces while I talk.

Let's look at some communication skills taught in Parenting 101. Learning to effectively communicate helps reduce frustration on the part of both parent and child.

- As often as possible, make direct eye contact when your child talks to you (not when you're driving, though). Next time you're in a crowd of people, watch how many parents enthusiastically talk into a cell phone but unenthusiastically interact with their children. Don't be that parent. Listen with your eyes *and* ears.

- To make sure you understand what your child is saying, rephrase their statements. You don't have to sound like a psychologist—simply say something like, "You really described that situation with Daniel in a clear way. I want to make sure I understand what you said: You think you'd enjoy soccer more if you could switch teams so that you are not always with Daniel." This gives your child a chance to agree with or clarify what you said.

- If your child shares a serious concern with you, try to keep your emotions from taking over. When your daughter tells you that Queen Bee Melissa is bullying her, it's natural to want to duct tape Melissa to the wall. But children need to express their feelings before a non-judgmental adult. If the matter is truly serious, of course you'll take immediate action. In most cases, however, all that's needed is your 100-percent attention for a few minutes. (I admit, I have a tendency to butt in with my well-meaning but unwanted advice. After all, we adults have all the answers, don't we? Many times Sondra has said, "Mom, I'm going to tell you something, but I don't want you to say a word until I'm completely through. And I'll let you know when I'm through." At which point I bite my cheek and try not to interrupt.)

- Remember the heartbreaking movie about a boy and his beloved dog called Old Yeller? Have you become an Old Yeller without the dog? We all yell occasionally. But too much yelling soon becomes ineffective. Instead of yelling, try stating what behavior you want. Screaming "Quit bugging your sister when she's talking!" goes unheard. Instead, state "Please listen when your sister talks." Instead of yelling "Don't run in the house!" try "Please walk when you're in the house." I guarantee you'll find it's more effective. Also, direct statements always work better than threats. Children understand—and will more likely respond positively to—a statement such as "Yes, you can go outside and play as soon as the paper and crayons are put away in the craft cupboard." Sure beats screaming, "Get those crayons picked up now or you'll never see them again!"

Silvana, I get the picture about communicating what I want my kids to do. Yet there are still times when I need to discipline my child. What works besides spanking or time-outs?

One family had an amazingly creative idea to encourage positive behavior. When a child talked back or was disrespectful, Mom or Dad would pantomime filming with a video camera while saying, "Take two." That meant the child had a quick chance to

"take two" and respond in a positive way. The scene might look
like this:

> **Mom:** Ashley, could you please bring in the last bag of
> groceries from the car?
> **Ashley:** No way! Let Emma do it. I'm tired of always
> having to do her jobs.
> **Mom:** (pretending she has a video camera and is
> recording the scene) Take two!
> **Ashley:** (knowing she answered inappropriately) Sorry,
> Mom. I'll get the groceries.

> *End of scene.*

Let children know that they have one chance to redo their
"scene." If they still are disrespectful, consequences follow. Here
are some other parent-tested ways to discipline children:

- Fighting with siblings is a common problem. One
  mom had a quick and simple rule: If siblings fought,
  they had to work on a chore—together. This meant a
  squabble over sharing a toy could result in a brother
  and sister jointly washing windows or cleaning the inside of a car. Most times siblings worked out the situation in order to avoid the double duty.

- At the beginning of each week, give each child a roll of
  dimes. The concept is simple: Obey the house rules and
  you keep the money. Children who argue, refuse to do
  chores and so on lose their dimes for each infraction.

- As often as possible, reward positive behavior. Compliment your child on remembering to feed the dog.
  Thank your daughter for sorting all the mismatched

socks. A few positive reinforcements go a long way toward avoiding bigger discipline issues.

Enough about discipline. Let's get back to fun topics like
crazy games, creative craft projects and some fun family trips.

And If You Still Don't Believe that Fun Makes a Difference . . .

Tailor consequences for your child. When Sondra was five, she
was enamored with the musical *Joseph and the Amazing Technicolor Dreamcoat*. She had seen the play (with Donny Osmond as
Joseph) and knew the score by heart. We had even gone to the
fabric store, picked out some colorful "technicolor" material
and sewed her a "dreamcoat," which she wore constantly. Now,
because Sondra was a very easy-going child, if we put her in
time-out as a discipline technique, she sat there happily and
sang Broadway musicals. One day, knowing I had to make an
impression on her because of something she had done, I re-
sorted to the most drastic discipline possible: I told her that if
she repeated the negative behavior, she would have to take off
her dreamcoat for 15 minutes. It worked!

6

Cheerful Chores?

Cleaning your house while your kids are still growing is like
shoveling the walk before it stops snowing.

PHYLLIS DILLER

It's a Saturday afternoon at your house. Which of the following
conversations take place between you and your children?

Conversation 1

Mom: Daniel, it's time for chores. Please empty the trash
and feed the dog.

Daniel: Of course, Mom. I'll get up from watching my favorite show on TV and empty the trash right away.
After I feed the dog, I'll brush him and take him for
a walk. Is there anything else I can do to help around
the house, my dear mother?

Conversation 2

Mom: Daniel, it's time for chores. Please empty the trash
and feed the dog.

Daniel: What? Why me? Why do I always have to take
out the gross trash? I did it last month. Sara can
feed the dog. She's not doing anything.

Mom: Daniel, we have an agreement that your chores
involve taking out the trash and seeing that the dog
is fed. Please start now.

Daniel: I don't remember any agreement. You're picking on me! Who came up with the idea of chores anyway? What a dumb idea.

If Conversation 1 is the standard at your house, then put this book away and nominate yourself for Parent of the Year. Most of us, however, feel like we've had Conversation 2 numerous times. There's something about the word "chores" that instantly causes friction between parent and child. Parents want children to learn responsibility and a sense of work ethic by helping around the house. Children simply want to avoid doing chores by any means possible. Certainly not a recipe for family harmony.

While Conversation 1 is probably a fantasy for most families, there *are* ways to make chores a bit more tolerable for children and the adults who nag the children. Perhaps some of the ideas in this Four-Week "Let's Get Started Doing Chores" Program will help ease "choreaphobia."

Silvana's Four-Week "Let's Get Started Doing Chores" Program

Week One

Chores can be a chore. As an adult, have you ever said, "It's such a chore to balance my checkbook"? Just the word "chore" has an unpleasant ring to it, doesn't it? After all, no one has ever said, "It's such a chore picking out chocolate in this Godiva Chocolate store."

This week, get your family to come up with a different word for "chores." Here are a few words to get you started:

- domestic requirements
- household duties
- spic-and-span time

- spit-spot time
- tasks

Take your family on a walk through the house and point out tasks that need to be done in order to keep the house from being condemned by the Health Department. For example, stand in the kitchen and ask, "What do you think needs to happen in this room on a regular basis?" Listen and make a list as family members talk about putting food away, closing cupboards, sweeping the floor, filling and emptying the dishwasher, wiping down the counters, cleaning spills inside the refrigerator, taking out the trash—and the list goes on. It might be the first time children come to understand what it takes to run a household.

Move on to a bathroom and repeat the list again. By the end of the house tour, your children will probably be exhausted just from hearing about all the possible chores they could be helping with. There will no longer be any need to point out that the adults do the majority of household work—the experience will speak for itself.

After the family meeting, write up a master cleaning list for each room. That way, everyone knows what needs to be done on a room-by-room basis. Post the list on the back of each room's door.

Week Two

At the beginning of the week, review the list of household tasks you made up during last week's tour. Ask children how some of these tasks can be divided up among family members. Let children pick one job they will agree to do. Write these down on a large piece of paper, complete with a time and date that the job will be done. When children have a say-so in selecting a household task, they are more likely to complete the chore.

Spend this week helping each family member do his or her assignment. If your four-year-old decides he wants to fold laundry, help him learn how. If your eight-year-old wants to vacuum, show her how to use the attachments for vacuuming stairs. Explain how to vacuum under furniture, as well as the need to lift up wastebaskets and throw rugs. Make sure your child understands each step so that you don't have to be the Chore Police and get upset when a job is left half-done.

Week Three

Evaluate what happened during Week 2. Did jobs get done on time? Were the jobs age-appropriate? Your five-year-old may have found that it's too hard to empty the dishwasher because she can't reach the upper shelves. Mix and match chores so that everyone has jobs they can do. (Notice I didn't say "has jobs they *love* to do." Most household duties aren't greeted with squeals of delight, but they should be suited to the age and ability of each family member.)

Week Four

Make it routine. This is the week to get the family settled into a regular routine of helping with household tasks. Make it a fun occasion. Compliment kids on the jobs they complete. Offer a surprise treat for kids who complete jobs with a minimum of moaning and complaining. Set up a reward system to help with motivation. (When I was in a boarding school run by nuns, they hid dimes in obscure places. When dusting or vacuuming, we'd get to keep any dimes we found. Just to keep the record straight, I only lasted two weeks at that school.)

These four weeks, I hope, have given you a good start toward making "cheerful chores" the norm in your household. As usual, though, the Four-Week Program, even with all its merits, has left some questions unanswered.

Ask the Fun Consultant

I just don't get it, Silvana. When I was little, I didn't have to walk 12 miles to school in a blizzard, but I was expected to set the table, hang up my clothes, feed the chickens and dust the living room. If I simply ask my son to hang up his backpack, he ignores me or makes a big scene. I'm almost hesitant to ask him to do something like take out the trash. He's also setting a bad example for his preschool-aged sister. How can I get him to help out?

As with most habits, it's best to start young. When kids are toddlers and preschoolers, they *want* to help—usually at those times when it's not terribly convenient for you. Yet the more we praise our children for helping, the more they'll see chores as a part of life, just like brushing teeth.

Of course, it's not too late for your son to pick up some good habits. Let him see that his contributions are important. If you ask him to set the table and he doesn't, sit down to eat at the empty table. Ask him what the family should do—there are no plates or silverware. It's obvious the family needs his help in order to eat dinner.

When your son complains that he has more chores than his sister, point out that he also has more privileges, such as later bedtimes and more freedom to go out with his friends.

You might consider getting a chore chart from www.kids contracts.com, which specializes in the pre- and early-teen ages. Another website, www.child.com, has free downloadable chore charts for other age groups.

Many parents find it helps to work alongside their child. Can you weed the garden together? How about you polishing the outside windows while he does the inside ones?

What about using a little fun and laughter to help your kids complete their household chores? Remember how Mary Poppins got the children to clean up their room? She sang "A Spoonful of Sugar Makes the Medicine Go Down." Her idea was that a bit of "sweetness" and downright frivolity made an ordinary experience enjoyable. So, when all else fails, threaten your children with a loud rendition of "A Spoonful of Sugar" if they don't do their chores.

Seriously, though—here are some great ways to add variety and fun to those dreaded domestic duties:

> If you've never visited a Montessori school, you might be shocked to observe children play with a puzzle and then put it back on the "puzzle" shelf. Next, that child gets crayons and markers, draws a picture and returns the craft supplies to the designated spot. Even more amazing is that no adult yells, "How many times do I have to tell you to put away your toys?" Children in Montessori schools are taught to be responsible for keeping the classroom neat by putting items back after using them.

- Many parents have success playing some loud music (Beach Boys' surfing hits are great) and having children complete specific chores before each song ends.

- Other parents assign chores and set a timer for 10 minutes. As soon as the timer goes off, children rotate jobs. Knowing a task ends in an allotted amount of time helps children feel that an end is in sight.

- Using small strips of paper, write out household tasks that need to be completed. Insert one strip of paper (the equivalent of one chore) into a balloon; then blow up the balloon. Repeat the process until all the chores are in midair. Then have family members pop two or three balloons . . . without using their hands! After popping the balloons, they complete the chore described on the rolled-up paper. If you have both older teens and little ones in your family, color-code the balloons so that younger children get age-appropriate chores. (*Caution*: If there is a toddler in the house, quickly pick up any popped balloon pieces to prevent him or her from putting the latex in his or her mouth.)

- Have each child decorate an empty soup can using markers and stickers. Once a month or so, designate Saturday morning as Chores in a Can Day. Ahead of time, write age-appropriate chores on slips of paper and place them in each child's can. Make it a fun experience by creating "nontraditional" chores such as "Have the dog chase you around the house two times," "Read a story to your little sister," "Vacuum the hall while singing 'Jingle Bells' " or "Sweep the garage wearing a silly costume." You'll get actual work done, but in a light-hearted way.

- Are there lots of small toys cluttering the floor? Give your child a pair of kitchen tongs and then keep time to see how long it takes him or her to pick up and put away 10 items. Let kids have a light-hearted competition to see who can pick up the most toys. The tongs transform an ordinary job into a game.

- If there's a major project to do, consider inviting another family to help. Two families raking leaves or organizing the garage creates an instant party. Be sure to help your friends at a later date.

- Get a set of index cards and write a chore on each card. Include a few highly coveted cards such as "Give your mom a hug" and "Watch TV for 30 minutes." Include

one grand prize card that reads, "No chores today."
Let children select two or three cards, and then have
them complete the tasks described.

- Younger children might like a reward chart kept in
their bedroom. When a child completes his or her chore,
add a glow-in-the-dark star to the chart. The child's
"reward" is seeing the glowing stars in his room at night.

- Walk through your house and see what child-friendly
items could help your children. Are there hooks available at a low level so that your child can easily hang up
her backpack and coat? Consider putting down a
large towel or sheet when your child plays with Legos,
then as he or she finishes, simply gather up the cor-
ners of the sheet and funnel the Lego pieces into a
storage container. How about labeling storage shelves
with pictures or words so that children can easily put
away toys in the proper place?

- This idea might be fun for parents rather than kids. One
mom with three children got tired of constantly nagging her children to pick up their toys. One day while
they were at school, she boxed up every toy, video game,
crayon and puzzle and took them to an understanding
neighbor for storage. Her children came home to a very
uncluttered house, and for an entire week they learned
what it was like to live in a toy-less house.

Chores, tasks, domestic duties—whatever you want to call
them—are a part of life . . . unless, of course, you are fabulously
wealthy and have cooks, gardeners and housekeepers. But until
you win the lottery, teach your children that chores are necessary but can also be fun. When you plan ahead and add a few
creative ideas, children soon learn that everyone needs to chip

in and help run the household. And then it won't be long until your family conversation will sound something like this:

> **Mom:** Emily, could you shake out the bathroom rugs?
>
> **Emily:** Of course, Mother. I'll gladly shake out the rugs. And I want you to relax today . . . I'll also clean the toilets, scrub the bathtubs and polish the mirrors. Can I get you a glass of lemonade before I start my chores?

Well, we can always dream, can't we?

And If You Still Don't Believe that Fun Makes a Difference . . .

Sondra is supposed to keep her room in a semi-clean state. Still, one day after repeated warnings to straighten things up, Allan and I took over. We walked into her room carrying large garbage bags and announced, "We're cleaning your room!" Ignoring her protests, we turned into the Two Musical House Cleaners, singing in dramatic style such profound lyrics as "Oh, my! There are so many shoes on the floor. That must mean Sondra has too many shoes. Let's put these four pairs in storage." The shoes were deposited in the garbage bags. The next chorus was, "Look at this—12 magazines on the floor. I think one magazine is enough, don't you?" Soon another bag was filled with magazines.

Within 15 minutes (and many verses later), we had 4 large bags filled with items from her bedroom floor. Again, with a comical yet triumphant flourish, we left her clean room, singing, "It should be easier for you to keep a clean room now that you don't have so many things. You can have these bags back after you keep your room clean for two weeks." Naturally, we took a bow after our Tony Award-winning performance. Sondra didn't give us a standing ovation. Yet one year later, all we have to say is "Do you want the Musical House Cleaners to clean your room?" and she races to her room, dragging the vacuum cleaner with her.

7

Crafts for the Un-Crafty

Every child is an artist. The problem is how to
remain an artist once we grow up.

PICASSO

It was the early summer of 1990. A time of innocence in the craft world. A time when I had the greatest intention of running high-quality, safe day camps in 10 locations throughout the city. I eagerly planned goofy games, trained staff and sought out creative activities.

While planning the craft program, I came across a book describing a great project called Asbestos Papier Mâché. The directions read, "Mix 5 pounds asbestos powder with 3 cups water to create the paste for papier mâché." Five pounds? Ha! I was the queen of papier mâché. I purchased asbestos in 25 pound bags. Then, with reckless abandon, I instructed 250 campers to mix asbestos and water so that they could make papier mâché creations.

Times have changed, and 25-pound bags of asbestos are no longer on my craft supply list. What hasn't changed is the need for children to express their creativity through arts and crafts projects. In today's high-tech world, many children miss out on the creative process of molding, shaping, painting and gluing. Holding on to a joystick or computer mouse is a sterile activity (yes, the video game manufacturers stress how children are developing hand-eye coordination while playing video games— but just watch kids develop hand-eye coordination as they string beads to make necklaces). When doing crafts, children are actively engaged in the activity, not staring blurry-eyed at a television screen.

Parents hear daily (sometimes dire and threatening) reminders about the importance of spending "quality time" with their children. Your nine-year-old will join a gang because you didn't bake cookies together on a weekly basis. Your preteen daughter will want to quit attending church because Mom had to work part-time. Parents want to have fun with their children but often lack the time and creative resources to plan "quality time."

Arts and crafts can play a vital role in establishing positive interaction with your children. Yes, arts and crafts! Now, don't worry that you'll have to be a Martha Stewart, with meticulously organized sequins that are color coordinated and sorted by size. Remember, the ideas in this chapter come without any pressure to create picture-perfect crafts. With crafts, the emphasis is on the *process*, not the *result*.

"But I'm not crafty," you moan. Never fear. Even if you don't know the difference between tacky glue and school glue, you can still get children involved in easy craft projects. These ideas are all designed to be the springboard for a relaxed, fun time with your children. If your daughter wants to make a purple six-eyed puppet, go for it! The world needs more purple six-eyed puppets. The simple act of sharing glue and laughing about crooked paint lines provides a natural avenue for establishing a strong parent-child relationship.

I can just hear some of your objections now:

"Crafts are too messy. I don't want glue on my furniture."
"My kids don't like crafts."
"Our budget doesn't allow for fancy craft supplies."

Sorry, but those excuses are overshadowed by the benefits children gain from making craft projects. Try this Four-Week

Program and see if your family doesn't turn into a group of craft-loving, hot-gluing artistic fanatics.

Silvana's Four-Week "Let's Get Started Crafting" Program

Week One

Forget all the preconceived ideas you have about crafts being too complicated or requiring imported rice paper and expensive professional-quality paints. For this first week, find a closet shelf or drawer—or even a large box—that can hold your craft supplies. Prepare a list that includes the following items:

- ❑ Buttons
- ❑ Cardboard tubes (from paper towels or toilet paper)
- ❑ Colored paper
- ❑ Crayons
- ❑ Empty yogurt containers or small boxes
- ❑ Fabric scraps
- ❑ Glitter
- ❑ Glue
- ❑ Markers
- ❑ Paint
- ❑ Paint brushes
- ❑ Popsicle sticks
- ❑ Stickers
- ❑ Tape
- ❑ Tissue paper
- ❑ Yarn

Send your children on an arts-and-crafts hunt through the house to gather the supplies you already have. After the craft supplies have been collected, see what basic items are missing. Are glue bottles dried out? Has the construction paper faded?

If needed, purchase a few more items so that you have a well-stocked craft box. (Many Dollar Stores now carry a large stock of crayons, foam pieces and even scrap-booking paper, so start there.)

Week Two

Start this week by getting the family together and suggesting a simple craft project: a paper chain. This colorful chain is easy for preschoolers, while older children can add their own elaborate designs. Instead of making the traditional red-and-green paper chain at Christmas, decorate one room in your house with some brightly colored, modern-art paper chains.

Cut various colors of construction paper into strips 3 inches wide and 8 inches long. Give each child 12 to 15 strips. Ask them to decorate the strips with assorted stars, sequins and paper scraps. Provide markers so that kids can embellish the strips even more. Staple or glue the strips to form a looped chain, just like you did in kindergarten. Hang the chain in a place where everyone can be reminded daily about their artistic abilities. Some families end up leaving the chain-making supplies on the table so that kids can add more links whenever they have time. Who knows—you may one day have a paper chain hanging throughout your entire house.

Week Three

Craft people are happy people, so this is an ideal week to make Happy Headbands. Cut strips of paper to make headbands, each of which should be approximately 4 inches wide by 24 inches long (you can also tape strips together to get the desired length). Don't staple the headbands into a loop yet—they're much easier to decorate when they're flat. Use sequins, stickers, paper scraps and shiny buttons to embellish the headbands. Glue strips from crepe paper rolls to the back so that the headband has "movement" when the children run. Show children how to wrap thin strips of paper around a pencil to form paper antennas.

When each headband has been decorated, "measure" the strip by holding it around the child's head and cutting/adding paper, if needed. Then staple the ends so that the headband sits firmly on the child's head.

After making your flashy headbands, try a game of "Follow the Leader Who Just Happens to Be Wearing a Fancy Headband." Select one child to wear his or her headband and be the leader. The rest of the group follows the actions of the leader. If the leader hops, the entire group hops. Take turns so that every child has a chance to wear his or her headband and be the leader.

Week Four

Hopefully your family is now getting crafty! In order to graduate from this program, you're going to make a very unique craft that is . . . get ready . . . *messy.* But the fun outweighs any hassle of cleaning up. In addition, your kids will think you're the coolest Fun-Filled Parent on the block.

Give each family member a clean raw egg. Use permanent markers to decorate (see, it's already fun just having the excitement of possibly cracking the egg). After eggs are decorated, help children poke a hole in one end with a sharp needle; the hole should be about the size of a dime. (Small nail scissors are ideal for cutting the hole.) When the hole is complete, place the egg over a bowl. Turn the egg over and poke a small hole in the opposite end. Blow hard into one end of the hole so that the yolk comes out of the large hole. Then rinse the egg well and let dry (to speed the drying process, place a hairdryer over the large hole). Repeat until everyone has a hollow egg.

While the eggs are drying, show children how to make confetti from tissue paper or construction paper. Help them cut paper into tiny, tiny pieces. When you have homemade confetti, the fun begins! Let children take turns dropping pieces of the confetti into the large hole of their egg. After all the eggs are confetti-filled, place a piece of tape over the hole.

Then proceed to explain that in some European countries, these eggs are used to celebrate New Year's. Invite an adult to come forward and face the group of children. Pretend it's New Year's Eve and say "Happy New Year!" as you break the egg over your volunteer's head. This is childhood humor at its best—there's something hysterically funny about seeing Mom or Dad get an egg cracked on their head and then covered with confetti. Take turns so that every person gets the thrill of having his or her colorful egg cracked over someone else's head.

Clean up is a breeze: Pick up the largest eggshell pieces and vacuum the confetti.

Now was that so hard? You didn't have to spend hours in preparation, and you certainly didn't need to sort your beads by size and color to be a successful crafter.

Ask the Fun Consultant

I don't know, Silvana. What's the purpose of doing crafts? Isn't it just busy work? Do kids really gain anything from doing an arts and craft project?

You might think crafts are just mindless activities, but children do learn valuable skills while doing crafts. For example, crafts help children learn to solve problems. Kids figure out what to do if there isn't enough red paper for their gigantic Valentine. Maybe they'll decide to make do with their white paper and use red paint. Such small decisions lay the foundation for solving more complex problems later on in life.

Often, as children try to solve problems, the results can be frustrating. Remember when you tried to deal with the class bully? It was scary and uncomfortable to find ways of dealing with the situation. With crafts, however, the problems are easier to manage. Children gain confidence in their problem-solving skills by starting small and working their way up.

One family tried to stuff a scarecrow as part of their fall decorations, but the straw kept falling out of the pant legs. One enterprising nine-year-old said, "Let's stuff my dance tights with straw and then put the tights inside the pants." That's creative problem solving!

Arts and craft projects encourage creativity. A child's typical day is made up of absolutes: They have to brush their teeth, put on a seatbelt, go to school, and so on. And most teachers don't encourage creativity when it comes to finding the answer to 6 + 7. When children create craft projects, they have the opportunity to add their personal touch to their creation. In the process, they gain valuable skills as they learn how to be creative. Consider this: Businesses encourage their employees to "think outside the box." In fact, many businesses now offer creativity training to their employees because they want more than just standard solutions to problems. So all that crafting might actually prove to be a great career move down the road.

Craft projects also help children gain self-confidence. Every school has their share of superathletes, stars of the school talent show and the all-around amazing kids with outgoing personalities. But what about kids who aren't athletically gifted and have a more reserved personality? Crafts are a perfect opportunity for these kids to display their special talents.

Experience with crafting results in children with creative minds, who are unafraid to think outside the box. Hey—they may even decorate their box.

My kids really do like to do crafts, but we never seem to have time to do those involved projects I see in magazines. My kids lose interest if they have to wait overnight for paint to dry or clay to harden. Any ideas for craft projects we can do in a limited amount of time?

Of course! So glad you asked. Here are some tried and true "speedy crafts" for those times when you want to spend time with your children yet don't have a whole afternoon to do a complicated project.

- Kool Kites: Cut a piece of construction paper into a kite shape. Save leftover pieces of paper to use as decorations. Set out an assortment of stickers and sequins to decorate your Kool Kite. Attach an 18-inch strip of crepe paper to the back—instant kite tail. Display your high-flying decoration on a wall in your home.

- Firecracker Picture: Set out pieces of dark blue or black construction paper. Cut an old Mylar balloon into strips and glue to the paper, representing fireworks. Add star stickers for an extra explosive effect.

- Sturdy Shakers: Cover a four- or five-inch-long cardboard tube with neon paper. Staple one end shut. Add one tablespoon of uncooked rice or popcorn. Here's the tricky part: Twist the open end in the opposite direction as the stapled end. This gives you a firm foundation for your shaker. Cut several 8-inch pieces of crepe paper or ribbons, then stick the ends inside the twisted tube and staple shut. Let children decorate the shaker with stickers and brightly colored paper scraps. Use the shakers as background music while singing your favorite songs.

- Something Ugly for a Change: Most crafts are cute or creative—this one won't be. Set out an assortment of craft odds and ends (this is a great chance to use up small pieces of paper, buttons, chenille stems, wiggle eyes, aluminum foil, small boxes, and so on). Ask the kids to make something ugly. They'll love making some strange monster puppets or weird sculptures.

- Crayon Rubbings: Give children an unwrapped crayon and some paper. Ask them to go around the house or outdoors and make rubbings of various items. Afterward, see if the rest of the family can identify the objects from the crayon marks on the paper.

- Magic Paint: Keep a jar of lemon juice handy. Let children draw pictures, using a cotton swab dipped in lemon juice as "paint." The paper looks blank. Have an adult hold the picture close to a lightbulb—the picture magically appears!

- Moving Painting: Take the idea of moving a paintbrush around on paper and turn it on its head. Have an adult hold a paintbrush (with paint on the tip) in a stable position. Children then take a piece of heavy paper or cardboard and move the paper back and forth over the brush to create a painting. This takes some getting used to!

- Colors of Emotion: Give each child paper and markers or crayons. Play short selections of various types of music. Ask children to color or paint how the music makes them feel.

- Construction Paper Sculpture: Cut paper into various strips, each anywhere from 3 to 8 inches long. The width can vary from 1 to 4 inches. Give each child a piece of brightly colored paper and 8 to 10 paper strips. Children can decorate the strips with shiny stickers and sequins. Show children how to make a 1-inch bend at the end of each paper strip. Dab glue on each end of the paper fold. Attach to a larger piece of construction paper, making an arch. Now continue adding glue to the folded ends, interconnecting the strips on the sculpture. Once the children understand the concept, they can construct this sculpture on their own. Older children enjoy making intricate designs with paper looping and spiraling in many directions.

You and your family have mastered Crafts 101. If you've discovered your "crafty side," go to any bookstore or library to find a wide assortment of craft books for more creative projects.

And If You Still Don't Believe that Fun Makes a Difference . . .

In our house, we solve 99 percent of our problems with a hot-glue gun. Broken toy? Fix it with the glue gun. Need to attach feathers to a chicken costume? Use the glue gun. Can't get a picture to hang straight? Add a drop of hot glue to the back of the frame. Let it cool and then hang; the dried dab of glue prevents the picture from slipping. Had a button fall off? What else? Attach it with a glue gun.

One day, I was doing a Sunday School craft workshop for adults. Naturally, I had the glue gun plugged in, ready to use. One woman cautiously asked, "I've never used a glue gun. Isn't it dangerous?" Sondra quickly walked over to the glue gun, held it in the air and announced, "I'm here to help anyone who doesn't know how to use a glue gun. Bring me your projects and I'll glue them for you." Five women walked over, grateful to have her glue their projects.

She was four years old.

8

Creating a Creative Family

Imagination is more important than knowledge.
EINSTEIN

I know at this point some of you are thinking that a few of these Fun-Filled Parenting ideas are a bit too loud, too messy, too rambunctious, too complicated, too weird and too time-consuming. Well, here come even more loud, messy, rambunctious and weird ideas, all designed to encourage your children to be creative.

As a professional speaker, one of my most requested topics is "Creativity: What Is It and Where Do I Get It?" Business leaders call me up and say, "I have intelligent employees, but they don't show many signs of creativity. People do their jobs adequately, just not with fresh insight and creative thinking." Given the importance of creativity in the work world, isn't it smart to see fostering creativity in your children as a good investment? (For them *and* for you—they get high-paying jobs so that they can buy you that deluxe RV.)

Many teachers also complain about their students' lack of creative thinking. One teacher said, "Kids today have parents helping them with homework, setting up play dates and solving their problems. These students know how to follow directions on a video game but get stymied when asked to make up an actual game using a ball and a jump rope."

There's no need for *you* to be stymied when it comes to creativity because you have . . . drum roll, please . . . the amazing Four-Week crash course in creativity.

Silvana's Four-Week "Let's Get Started on Creativity" Program

Week One

One aspect of creativity involves "embellishing" an idea. Instead of simply serving tacos for dinner, embellish the Mexican theme. Play Mexican music and find an easy recipe for flan, a traditional Mexican desert. Give children paper and ask them to create placemats that use the colors of the Mexican flag (see, even a little research is involved). What Spanish words do you know? After dinner, find a hat and make up your own version of the Mexican Hat Dance. Look what just happened. You were creative! Throughout the week, continue to look for ways to "embellish" other ordinary activities.

Week Two

Many creative people are known as "twisted thinkers." They take an ordinary idea or activity and give it their own creative twist. In England, for example, Michael Gill knew that many preachers wanted to preach but didn't have churches. He designed an inflatable church with Gothic arches, a blow-up organ, polyvinyl pulpit and even seating for 35.[1] Now traveling ministers simply find an electrical outlet, inflate their church and start preaching to whoever shows up. How's that for a twist on a traditional church-building program?

Encourage your children to be flexible in their thinking. Serve pancakes for dinner. Ask your son to list 25 uses for a spoon. Instead of simply driving your daughter to dance class, get twisted! Ask her to come up with another form of transportation. Maybe you'll end up spending 35 minutes taking the bus or simply getting a ride with a friend. The point is to look at a situation and ask, "How can we use flexible, twisted thinking in this situation?"

Week Three

Take some risks. When Microsoft interviews potential employees, they ask the candidate, "Tell us about a time you took a risk at work." Microsoft encourages risk-taking, even if it means making a mistake. Why? Because sometimes a mistake can lead to a creative multibillion-dollar idea.[2]

Your family is comfortable going to their usual restaurants and community haunts. This week, take a risk and attend a community event that is a new experience for your family. Who knows what you'll discover at the Mexican Hairless Dog Show or the exhibition of Bowling Balls Through the Ages? Simply look through a local newspaper for community events. You're sure to find something of interest.

Don't hesitate to ask other people for help in your creativity campaign. If you're at the bowling alley, ask the manager to show your children how he drills holes in bowling balls. Go to an ethnic restaurant and ask for a sample of the most unique food they serve. Take a risk and sign your family up for a free class in snowshoeing.

Week Four

Teach your children a new skill this week. Has your 10-year-old ever used a hammer and nails? Build a wobbly birdhouse or a fort. Has your six-year-old climbed a tree? Find a tree with sturdy branches

> Think about the ways Jesus modeled creativity. He preached from a boat, not behind a pulpit. He used object lessons like empty fish nets and fig trees to make His point.

and teach her how to step from limb to limb. Encourage your kids to do things they've never done before. Remember that creative thinkers are open to learning new skills.

Bob Winters, a fifth-grade teacher in Bellingham, Washington, told his students, "This year we'll be doing many creative things. Since you'll be learning new skills, I've decided to teach myself to ride a unicycle. By the last week of school, I hope to be able to ride around the gym." Naturally, his students responded by eagerly learning new skills by themselves. (And, yes, Bob did make it around the gym on the unicycle, supported by his cheering students.) If you don't want to buy unicycles for the family, find some other skills to teach your children. Maybe this is the time to show off your hidden yodeling talent!

As you can see from this Let's Get Started program, creativity takes many forms. One mother, tired of her 10-year-old son, Johnny, constantly forgetting his lunch, used creative thinking after nagging failed. She received the usual call from Johnny at school saying, "Mom, please bring me my lunch; I promise I'll never forget it again." Cheerfully, she reassured him his sack lunch would be delivered promptly. And deliver it she did.

She transformed the ordinary brown sack (acceptable to pre-teens everywhere) into a preschool work of art. The sack was adorned with stickers, happy faces and, of course, "Mommy Loves You!" written with a bold red marker. For extra creativity, she attached several balloons and hand-delivered it to his classroom. Thanks to Mom's creativity, Johnny never forgot his lunch again.

Ask the Fun Consultant

Silvana, I hear so many people talking about "thinking outside the box," but I'm not terribly creative. I'd much rather follow the rules so that everything stays as even-keeled as possible. Yet I see my kids just going along with the crowd and not thinking for themselves. What are some ways I can encourage my kids to think and act creatively?

Remember when your mother would ask, "So if all your friends jumped off a bridge, would you jump off also?" At which point you felt inclined to mutter, "Yes," but you knew that was the wrong answer. Just as parents of old, we don't want our children following the crowd. Too often the crowd is heading in the wrong direction. But take heart—there are many ways to develop creative thinking in your child's life.

Try some of these very basic activities that teach your child valuable life skills in a creative way.

- What's the difference between the White and Yellow Pages? Ask your preteen daughter, "Let's say my skin breaks out in pimples. How would I find the phone number of a skincare doctor?" See if she knows the term "dermatologist." What happens when she looks up "doctor"? (Doctors are usually listed under "physicians.") Does your son want a pair of high-priced tennis shoes? Have him look up the number of three athletic shoe stores and ask for the price of his desired shoes. For some children, learning to use the phonebook can be a daunting task. Offer encouragement and praise because they are going out of their comfort zone.

- Do you get tired of having children answer questions with a grunt or "Whatever"? Lead by example when it comes to outstanding communication. Speak in full sentences when talking to adults. Incorporate some public-speaking skills into everyday conversation. Role-play situations that help children learn how to give polite replies to adults. Make up silly situations so that children can relax as they learn to add a few words to their normal one-word answers. Act out "normal" and "creative" conversations that demonstrate the importance of talking in full sentences. The results are hilarious when you exaggerate the responses. For example, you might announce to the family, "Let's listen in on a conversation between Jacob and his soccer coach before he knew how to talk in complete sentences."

> **Coach:** Hey, Jacob. We missed you at practice yesterday. Were you sick?
> **Jacob:** Ya.
> **Coach:** Are you feeling well enough to play today?
> **Jacob:** I dunno.
> **Coach:** Do you want to try to play?
> **Jacob:** I guess.

Then role-play the dramatic improvement in conversation when children speak in full sentences.

> **Coach:** Hey, Jacob. We missed you at practice yesterday. Were you sick?
> **Jacob:** Well, I had a stomachache. I think it was from eating my mom's meatloaf.
> **Coach:** Are you feeling well enough to play today?
> **Jacob:** Sure. I took Alka Seltzer and now I feel great. I just won't eat my mom's meatloaf anymore.

When you keep things light, children learn a valuable creative communication tool.

- Write a thank-you letter—yes, an actual handwritten letter on real paper that goes inside an envelope. The average 11-year-old has no idea how to address an envelope. Employers say only 5 percent of job applicants write a thank-you note after an interview. Your children aren't applying for a job, but they can learn the importance of writing a thank-you letter. How about thanking a soccer coach, violin teacher or even a Scout leader? Children learn the mechanics of writing a letter, and the recipient gets a pleasant handwritten surprise. Girls might enjoy decorating their paper with stickers and rubber stamps.

• Rearrange some furniture. For a simple exercise in creativity, get the family together for 15 minutes to move the living room furniture around. Don't worry if the "feng shui" isn't there. Leave the new floor plan for a few days. As you sit and talk with each other, see if the new arrangement works. What's it like to have Dad's favorite chair directly in the center of the living room? What happens when the couch faces a wall instead of a window?

• Give your children an ordinary object and have them brainstorm "alternative" ways to use it. Georges Hemmerstoffer, a publisher in Germany, prints novels and poetry on toilet paper. That way he knows the books will get read![3] What can you do with an empty bucket, an old toothbrush or a broken lawn mower?

• Organize a Tall Tales Contest. Ahead of time, cut out an assortment of pictures from a magazine. The pictures can range from an ordinary-looking car to a nose on a magazine cover. Each family member randomly selects a picture and then makes up an outrageous Tall Tale about their picture.

• Pass around a bag filled with odds and ends such as a dirty sock, a hair ribbon or broken toy. Have children reach in the bag, pull out an item and instantly make up an infomercial. You'll get some crazy sales pitches!

· Plan an International Night using books from the library as a resource for recipes, traditions and mini-geography lessons. One family held a German evening by making pretzels while listening to polka music. The evening ended with a sauerkraut-eating contest.

· You've probably watched *Extreme Makeover: Home Edition*, in which a worthy family gets a dream house. The children arrive to find themed bedrooms reflecting their interests. Most people don't have the budget that the *Extreme Makeover* crew does, so use creativity instead. Have children design their own dream rooms using pictures from old magazines. Take time to let each child explain their designer masterpiece.

· Feel free to dream. Encourage your children to think about a dream they have. Do they want to go skiing in Switzerland? Get their own horse? Swim with the dolphins? Put some action behind those dreams. Show children how to use the Internet or toll-free 800 numbers to get brochures and other information.

· When talking with your children, try using open-ended questions as often as possible. A closed question is, "Sam, should you hit your brother when he takes the crayons?" Sam will obviously answer, "No." An open-ended question such as, "Sam, what are two things you can do when your little brother takes the crayons?" allows him to think of creative solutions.

· Looking for a unique way to spend one-on-one time with your elementary-aged child? Invite him or her to go on a Mystery Field Trip with you. Here's the catch:

The activity has to be something neither one of you have done before. There's a bit of risk involved in attending a senior citizens' breakfast or watching a student ballet production. The fun comes in being together with your child as you both participate in a "new" activity. Local newspapers always list upcoming community events such as author book signings, community fundraisers and special events. One mother, striving to be a Fun-Filled Parent, took her eight-year-old son to the grand opening of a new convention center, which turned out to be a memorable event. The visit began by eating cake and getting free T-shirts. Then a group demonstrating team-building activities put the mother and son in Velcro suits and had them jump against a Velcro wall where they stuck like Spider-Man. Now that's a mother-son bonding experience!

Creativity doesn't have to be a formal "We'll be creative on Tuesdays and Thursdays" type of philosophy. Often creativity is simply pausing a split second before taking action and asking, "Is there a more creative way to handle this situation?" Let me illustrate.

One family felt so overscheduled that they seldom had quiet time together. That changed when the parents set a timer for 20 minutes each evening and the family simply sat next to each other in the living room, silently reading. Not very exciting stuff. Yet at the next parent-teacher conference, the teacher told the parents their son had shared in class that the best part of his day was sitting next to Dad as they both read. Who says creativity needs to be messy and flamboyant? (Okay, maybe I did . . .)

Sometimes the best catalyst for creativity is giving children unstructured time. When children race from school to violin lessons to karate class, there's little need to think creatively. Give children free time and—after they complain about being bored—they'll soon develop plenty of creative ideas.

A college student remembers the year she was nine and suffered an agonizing blow to her ego. She wanted to play the role of Clara in her dance recital's production of *The Nutcracker* (along with 40 other little ballerinas). Her dad put creativity to work and bought his daughter a sparkly tutu at a discount store. Then he arranged for Grandma and Grandpa to come over and watch a unique performance of *The Nutcracker*, starring their granddaughter. "My dad even put on long underwear to look like tights and then danced with me, lifting and twirling me in the air as if I were a real ballerina," she recalls. Who knew creativity involved long underwear?

And If You Still Don't Believe that Fun Makes a Difference . . .

When Sondra was four, our normally easy-going daughter announced at bedtime, "I'm not putting on my pajamas and I'm not going to bed. So there!"

Allan calmly walked over to her dresser and removed two nightgowns and three sets of pajamas. He carefully placed the items in a large circle on the living room floor. Sondra watched cautiously, wondering if this was some sort of ploy (of course it was).

When he was finished with his arrangements, her father finally said, "Remember when you went to the preschool carnival cake walk? You had to walk from number to number until the music stopped. This is a pajama walk. I'll play some music and you walk from pajama to pajama. You get to wear whatever you're standing on when the music stops. We'll practice a few times, of course."

Suddenly a potentially negative situation turned into five minutes of fun as Sondra marched from pajama to pajama, delighting in the whole experience. Soon she was tucked into bed, wearing the special pajamas that "destiny" had chosen when the music stopped. Creativity put our daughter to bed with smiles and kisses rather than tears and heartache.

Notes

1. "Inflatable Church Brings New Meaning to Mobile Wedding." http://www.inflat ablechurch.com/mainpage.htm (accessed February 2008).
2. Bob Nelson, "Recipe for Good Management: Allow Employees to Take Initiative," WebProNews, April 15, 2002. http://www.webpronews.com/topnews/2002/04/15/ recipe-for-good-management-allow-employees-to-take-initiative (accessed March 2008).
3. "Roll of Honor," The Times of India, October 14, 2002. http://timesofindia.indi atimes.com/articleshow/25081453.cms (accessed February 2008).

9

Homework Hostess Reduces Homework Hassles

Home computers are being called upon to perform many new functions, including the consumption of homework formerly eaten by the dog.
DOUG LARSON

Wouldn't it be great if homework were never an issue? Imagine the joy of having our children walk through the front door after school with the words, "No need to make me a snack, Mom. I'm too excited to get started on my homework. Mrs. Connors assigned a 10-page paper on the Franco-Prussian War. What a great topic! I think I'll add some graphs and charts, too. I can't wait to get started!"

Instead, you probably dread homework as much as your children. Some school districts actually have had parents lobby for no homework, especially in the elementary grades. Many schools now have policies stating that no homework should be assigned over the weekend. Then, of course, there are those parents who urge teachers to pile on more homework in an effort to help students improve their test scores.

When our older daughter, Trina, was in fifth grade, she had a teacher who assigned homework seven days a week. Every day, Trina and her classmates—in addition to completing regular math and science homework—were supposed to read for 30 minutes and then write a one-page summary. Now, I'm all for reading, but having this assignment *every day* during the school year seemed a bit much. Finally I met with the teacher and told her that I and many other parents felt the homework was excessive, especially over the holidays. She grudgingly agreed to let students skip the assignment over Thanksgiving. (That's something they could be grateful for!)

Imagine my surprise when a mother called and indignantly told me I had been out of line in asking for a reduction in homework. Her daughter, it seems, literally raced home and began the reading and writing homework assignment because it was the high point of her day.

In most cases, some homework is sure to be a part of your child's after-school world. The National PTA and the National Education Association recommend students should receive no more than 10 minutes of homework per grade level per night (all subjects combined). That is, first graders can do up to 10 minutes, third graders up to 30 minutes, and so on.[1]

But no matter how much or how little homework your kids bring home, there's still the issue of getting it done. How do you handle the emotional toil involved in trying to get kids to do their homework?

Yes, you could seek counseling, but let's keep that as a last resort. How about trying this Four-Week "Let's Get Started with Homework Help" Program?

Silvana's Four-Week "Let's Get Started with Homework Help" Program

Week One

Get your children involved in coming up with a solution for reducing homework hassles. Do they need a designated workspace? Is the TV or music too distracting? What do they consider the best time to begin their homework? Listen to their input and work together to implement a few ways to maintain peace in the house after school.

Week Two

Use this week to set up Homework Central. Have the kids help make signs that read "Time to Study," "Genius at Work," and "The student that studies gets to play basketball." Make sure each child has an uncluttered desk or work area stocked with pencils, rulers and paper. For a treat, give each child an inexpensive desk organizer so that he or she can always find that elusive yellow highlighter. Help children set up an area that has good lighting and is free from distractions. Having the TV blaring while learning multiplication tables isn't the best combination.

One first-grader was delighted to have his very own "office": a large refrigerator box. He decorated the inside by coloring walls and adding dinosaur stickers. Then he did his homework on a lapboard surrounded by comfy pillows.

Week Three

Your kids have a *place* to study—now make sure they know *when* to study. Set a definite time when the TV is turned off, the answering machine is on, and the kids are at their desks. Some families find that getting homework done right after school works best. Your children may work better right after dinner but before they get too tired. Find what works best for your children and stick to that schedule throughout the week. If a child claims he has no homework, wonderful! He or she can still spend 20 minutes or so reviewing spelling words, reading a book or cleaning out that backpack.

Week Four

As an added incentive to get children in the routine of homework, let them see the adults in the family doing their own type of homework. Sit next to your children and pay bills, balance the checkbook, write a letter or simply read the paper. Having you in close proximity helps children stay focused and allows

them to see the "real world" applications of what they're studying. One family designates 30 minutes every evening when the
entire family sits at the kitchen table; kids do homework while
Mom and Dad do household bills or cut interesting articles
from magazines, which they later share with the whole family.

Homework gives children a sense of independence—in the process, it also makes them responsible for their own study habits.
Which is a good thing. After all, you don't want to be helping
your daughter with her college calculus do you? (Do you even
remember how to do college calculus?) So the key for you to remember is that your job is to foster that independence, that
sense of responsibility. And lucky for you, here are some help-
ful ideas to help you do just that.

- Consider yourself a Homework Hostess, offering
  friendly assistance. It's fine to bring your child a dic-
  tionary, but there's no need to look up the 15 words
  on his or her vocabulary list. One mom said, "I try to
  show my children I support their homework efforts,
  but I'm not doing their homework. When my daughter was writing a report on Africa, I bought her a set of
  jungle animal stickers. She used these to decorate the
  cover of her report. This way, I conveyed I was a proper
  Homework Hostess without spending hours looking
  up historical facts about Africa!"

- You are not the Homework Police, monitoring every
  sugar cube your son uses to build his replica of an
  igloo. If the igloo is lopsided, call it a new style of ar-
  chitecture and let your son figure out how to create a
  dome. In the same way, try to avoid threats like, "If
  you don't get this homework done, you'll flunk third
  grade, which means you'll never get to high school,

which means you'll never get a good job—and you'll be living at home the rest of your life."

- Keep a calm attitude as your daughter rants, "This homework is so hard! I'll never get it done!" Children like to display their theatrical ability while doing spelling worksheets. Don't escalate the situation by getting upset yourself. When children see their dramatic pathos has little effect on you, they'll concentrate more on actually doing their homework than on creating a scene. (Of course, when their assignments have been completed, feel free to offer to play a game of charades with them to provide an outlet for their dramatic abilities.)

- Be aware of resources available for those sticky homework dilemmas. Many school districts sponsor homework hotlines that let children get help in finding all sorts of useful information, such as the number of castles perched along the Rhine River. Other resources are:

  www.homeworkcentral.com
  www.kidsclick.org
  www.homeworkspot.org
  www.homeworkhelp.about.com

- If your child consistently forgets his or her homework assignment, work out a plan with the teacher. Have your child write down all assignments and get the list signed by the teacher before coming home. That way you know your child knows his assignments (now if you can just get them to remember to bring home the signed list!).

- Help children break down their assignments. Sometimes kids get so overwhelmed at the thought of "hours and hours" of homework that they can't focus.

Show your daughter how to make a checklist of assignments. It might read like this:

❏ Write spelling words five times each.
❏ Do page 22 in math book.
❏ Read pages 56-58 in history book.

Then ask your child which assignment she wants to do first. If math is her most difficult subject, suggest she do half the math problems, then her spelling words and then back to the math. Offer to listen to her as she reads the history pages to you. Many mothers find they can catch up on the ironing as their children read to them.

· Some children respond well to a homework contract. Type up a formal-looking contract that has guidelines developed by you and your child. Include items such as: time homework begins, where homework takes place, what to do if your child needs help, rewards for accomplishing tasks, and so on. Then post the signed contract in a prominent place to remind your son or daughter about his or her commitments.

Ask the Fun Consultant

Silvana, getting my daughter to do her homework every night has turned our house into a center for screaming, threats and tossed pencils. She doesn't have that much to do, yet it drags on for hours. How can I get her to sit down and just get it done?

Your daughter may be reacting to an overbooked schedule. How would adults feel if they put in a long day at the office and then trudged home, knowing they had to complete another hour or two of paperwork? Maybe your daughter needs to have complete "down time" when she gets home. Try not to schedule any after-school activities so that she has a chance to unwind. Give her a healthy snack and maybe read a book together. Then let her find something to do that doesn't require anyone giving instructions. If children first have unstructured time available to them, they're much more likely to have a better attitude when it comes to getting homework completed.

Silvana, I like your ideas about how to take the stress out of homework. Now it boils down to this: Should I reward my kids for doing their homework? Sometimes I get desperate and say things like "I'll take you out for ice cream as soon as you get this worksheet done." Lately all I'm doing is buying them toys and taking them places as a reward for doing regular homework.

Your gut reaction is right: Kids don't need to get rewards for doing what the teacher asks. Does your boss take you out to lunch because you turned in your weekly report on time? Probably not. However, healthy workplace environments do have ways to motivate employees, through raises, time off and bonuses. In the same way, try to incorporate motivational rewards to get children used to doing homework.

One mother used a unique tool to encourage her daughter, who was in second grade, to complete homework in a neat and timely fashion. Because her daughter had a close relationship with her grandmother, Mom would say, "You're really working hard on that math sheet. As soon as the teacher corrects it, I'll send it to Grandma. She'll be so proud that you are learning how to do those hard math problems." Grandma, of course, was thrilled to get the homework and praised and encouraged her granddaughter. (FYI: High-school seniors are seldom motivated to do extra research on a physics paper in hopes of getting a phone call from Grandma. Make age-appropriate choices when it comes to motivation.)

You can make the homework experience pleasant by offering a chance to "spin the spinner" when assignments have been completed. Make a homemade spinner, similar to ones found in many board games. On the circle surrounding the spinner, list various "rewards" children receive, such as "Stay up 15 minutes past bedtime," "Mom makes your bed tomorrow," "Take a bike ride with Dad after school," "Two extra stories at bedtime tonight." As soon as a child completes his or her homework, he or she gets to spin the spinner.

Some children respond well to "racing the timer." Give your child an appropriate length of time to complete his or her homework. Set a timer and see if your child is able to complete the assignments (accurately) before the timer goes off. If he or she beats the clock, offer to play a game or give him or her a few extra minutes of TV time. The key here is to show your child that homework doesn't have to drag on all night.

In some cases, parents need to admit that the power struggle to have kids do homework is too intense—sometimes creative help is needed. One mom tried endlessly to get her third-grade son to focus on doing his homework. She finally hired a seventh-grade neighbor to do 30 minutes of *his* homework while sitting next to her son (who, it was hoped, would also be doing his homework). The teenager served as a positive role model to the younger boy, who cheerfully completed his work without complaining. The payoff was a quick basketball game between the two boys. And because the seventh-grader was getting paid, you can bet he made an effort to set a good example and did his homework without complaining.

Last but not least, don't think *you* can get off the hook without a homework assignment. One elementary school principal told his parents, "I'm giving every one of you a nightly home-work assignment. Studies show one of the best indicators of children succeeding in school is having parents read to them. Your assignment is to read enthusiastically to your children for 20 minutes a day. Now go home and do your homework!"

And If You Still Don't Believe that Fun Makes a Difference . . .

Sometimes providing a "twist" on an ordinary assignment helps children do homework—like the time Allan helped Sondra study for a test on the Pilgrims. He found a big box and covered it with plain paper. Then he simply said, "Tell me everything you know about the Pilgrims, and I'll write it on this side of the box." Sondra rattled off the facts. Then he suggested they look at her history book and notes and add more information on the other side of the box. Soon she had a box covered with dates and historic events.

Sure, the same thing could be done with a piece of paper, but the box got her actively engaged in studying for her test. (By the way, did you know that the first national Thanksgiving was celebrated in 1777?)

Note

1. Cathy Vatterott, "Mom and Dad Aren't Taking Algebra This Year: Hints to Help Reduce Homework Stress, National PTA Parent Resources." http://www.pta.org/ pr_ magazine_article_details_1133559366703.html (accessed March 2008).

10

Make It Fun, Make It Simple

You will always be your child's favorite toy.

Vicky Lansky

Have you ever stood at the grocery store checkout counter and glanced at the headlines on magazines? I'm not talking about the captions that read "Mother Gives Birth to Two-Headed Triplets!" or "Is Your Child's Teacher an Alien from Mars?" No, I mean captions that say, "225 Ways to Make Your Child's Birthday Extra Special," "134 Ways to Decorate Cupcakes with Your Child" and "101 Games for Rainy Day Fun." If you happen to glance at the articles, you'll notice extensive directions that involve numerous trips to the store for supplies. The activities require hours of preparation—just so you and your cherub can decorate a cake to look like Cinderella's castle, complete with miniature imported stained glass windows.

Is that practical in today's fast-paced world? Of course not. Look over the following ideas and see how easy it is to have down-to-earth fun with your children. Best of all, there's little preparation required and you'll find most supplies are things you already have in your house.

We'll start with a simple Four-Week Plan. Soon your home will be known as the house where fun abounds!

Silvana's Four-Week "Let's Get Started with Quick and Simple Fun" Program

Week One

At least three mornings this week, surprise your children by dressing up in a funny costume and waking them up by chanting this clever little ditty:

> See the pretty flowers lift their faces to the sun!
> It's wake-up time! It's wake-up time!
> Aren't you glad God gave you wake-up time?

Act as if it's a normal occurrence for you to wake your children while you dance about, wearing a purple wig, fluorescent sunglasses and a fluffy square-dance petticoat.

Week Two

Your children are beginning to see a new side of their parents. This week, as they arrive home from school, have the front of the house decorated with balloons and streamers. Add a sign that says, "Welcome Home, Johnson Kids! We think you're great! Love, Mom and Dad." Have a special snack prepared. If possible, buy a new game or puzzle and take a few minutes to play together before the normal routine of homework and dinner prep begins.

Week Three

When the family is all together, announce that it's time to play Sprinting Ducks. (By this time, your children will probably be really wondering what happened to their previously "normal" parents.) Pick an area of the house that has a door with wall space on both sides of it. All family members sit inside the room, a few feet back from the open door. Each person holds foam balls, ping pong balls or small pillows (any item is fine as long as it's soft—one family even plays this game using all the Beanie Babies that clutter their house).

Pick a family member to stand in the hall, out of sight. His or her goal is to pretend to be one of those mechanical ducks at the carnival shooting gallery. The "duck" has to quack and waddle like a duck to the other side of the door. Of course, as the duck waddles past the door, family members toss soft items at him or her. Take turns so that everyone gets to be the duck. There's something quite amusing about seeing an adult quacking like a duck, throwing his or her body past a doorway to avoid getting hit by a Beanie Baby octopus.

Week Four

Are you seeing how easy it is to have spontaneous fun with your family? Here's an activity that will provide your family with a toe-tickling experience. Have everyone take off their shoes and socks. Take a look at the bottom of your toes. See how they look like little faces? It's time to give those faces some personality. Using washable markers, have pairs of family members draw faces on the bottom of their "coloring" partner's toes (if someone is extra ticklish, he or she will have a hard time holding still as his or her toes are decorated). When finished, take turns admiring everyone's smelly masterpieces.

Ask the Fun Consultant

Silvana, isn't it kind of silly to paint feet and dress up in costumes? Won't my kids lose respect for me as a parent?

Actually, your children will have more respect for you. By laughing together, you are creating a warm, positive relationship with your kids. Think about a time you and some friends got together and reminisced about "the good old days." Remember how you laughed about sneaking boys into the all-girls dorm at college? (Don't let your kids know you were so wild.) You felt closeness with your friends because of that great memory. In the same way, you are creating wonderful memories for your children. In a few years will they say, "I remember how my mom always nagged us about keeping our elbows off the table," or will they say, "I remember how my mom made a fort under the kitchen table where we read books together"? We talk about the importance of creating positive memories for our children. How can we get those memories if we don't do fun things now?

As parents, we can take an ordinary experience and make it fun, which in turn fosters a stronger relationship with our children. Maggie Scarf, in her book *Intimate Worlds: Life Inside the Family*, writes, "A common trait of dysfunctional families is a tremendous lack of humor—a deadly seriousness."[1]

Okay, Silvana, I know now that it's important to do quick and fun activities with my children. But just what exactly can I do?

So glad you asked! Just look over these ideas. They're perfect for those times you have an extra few minutes and want to have fun with your kids rather than fold laundry.

- *Daily Fun Master*. Assign each family member the job of coming up with a 5 to 10 minute family activity each day. Your preschooler might organize a game of Hide and Seek, while your teen might invite everyone to listen to his latest CD. The idea is to give family members responsibility for creating family fun. Dad or Mom could prepare an interactive family devotional that consists of more than reading a Bible verse and praying.

• *Crazy Clothes.* Take turns dressing as other family members for dinner. Mom dresses toddler style and Dad gets to look like a 13-year-old. Don't forget to take pictures!

• *Silly Duck-Duck-Goose.* Duck-Duck-Goose isn't just for little kids. This game can be played with family members or friends. Instead of the traditional game, add some creativity by changing focus. Fill a cup with cotton balls. Then have "It" walk around the circle, lightly resting the cup on top of each child's head while saying, "Plop, Plop, Plop . . . Drop!" At this point, he or she drops the cotton balls on another child's head. This produces screams of laughter from the group. Continue by filling the cup with confetti, feathers or a few ping-pong balls. For extra fun, try adding two tablespoons of water to the cup and saying "Dry, Dry, Dry . . . *Wet!*" at which point the designated child gets a little water poured on his or her head. This will elicit lots of giggles from the group.

• *Just Like Noah.* The next time it rains, give this familiar Bible story new meaning. Find a book about the story or read about Noah in the Bible. But wait! You won't simply read from the comfort of your home. Put on some boots and raincoats, and grab an umbrella. Take a walk with your family, noticing how different everything looks when it's wet. Point out mud puddles and raindrops dripping from plants. Listen to the sound of rain hitting the sidewalk. What happens when a car drives through the mud puddle next to you? Stick out your tongues and try to get a drink from raindrops. Bring your dog along. What does wet fur smell like?

Then find a safe place to stop and read the story of Noah's ark while standing under an umbrella. Help children imagine what it would be like to have rain for 40 days and 40 nights. The ark probably had some roof leaks. What would it smell like inside, with the wet fur from lions, bears and giraffes? After reading the story, walk home in the rain and then enjoy some hot chocolate.

• *Terrific Tails.* Looking for a fast-paced game that does not take much space? Try a quick round of Terrific Tails. Designate a circle about 10 feet in diameter, inside the house or out. Make sure the area is free from any items on the floor. You don't want to trip over someone's shoe or a rock. Cut two ribbons or crepe paper streamers, each about 24 inches long. Select a partner and have each person tuck 5 to 6 inches of ribbon in the back waistband of his or her pants. Have the partners go back into the center of the circle, hands on their heads. When someone says "Go!" each person quickly turns and tries to grab the tail of his or her partner, while staying within the circle. This results in some silly maneuvering as each person tries to contort his or her body to keep that tail out of reach. As soon as one person grabs a tail, he or she gets to challenge another competitor. Adults are amazed at the workout they get from playing this game with their children.

• *William Tell Target.* You probably have heard the story about William Tell. Because of a disagreement with the king, he was forced to shoot an apple off his son's head with an arrow. (Don't worry; you're not going to use a bow and arrow on your child!) Ask your child to stand against a wall and balance an apple on his or her head (this is harder than it sounds—apples are wobbly). When the apple is balanced, stand about 5 feet away from your child. Toss a cotton ball at your child's head in an attempt to hit the apple. How many tries does it take? Again, this is one of those activities that sounds boring on paper but elicits screams and cheers from your kids. Aren't you glad you're not using a bow and arrow? Now let your kids try to hit an apple on *your* head. If you are brave, allow them to toss a small, wet sponge.

· *Old-Fashioned Pillow Fight.* In *The Sound of Music*, Maria helps the children overcome their fear of thunder and lightning with a pillow fight. No need for a storm to surprise your children with a playful whack with a pillow.

· *Let's Pretend.* The Chinese have a belief that you will get good luck if you set an animal free. Have each family member pretend to have a "captured" animal. Describe the animal as other family members guess what it is. Let your animal go free, and get ready for good luck.

· *Crazy Alphabet Race.* Have each family member select a random letter from the alphabet. On "Go!" everyone has to race through the house and collect five items beginning with his or her designated letter. (We played this last week, and Sondra brought the entire disconnected VCR because her letter was *V.*)

· *Oscar Mayer.* Each year, the Oscar Mayer Company sponsors a nationwide search to find someone to sing their famous jingle. Video each family member give their most creative rendition of singing the famous song, which begins, "Oh, I wish I were an Oscar Mayer Wiener . . ." Who knows? If you submit the

finished product, one of you just might become a
national winner!

• *Let's March.* Play some John Philip Sousa or other
marching music. Designate a 30 to 60 minute time pe-
riod in which family members have to march wherever
they go in the house.

• *Guess That Taste.* Set out an assortment of food such as
raw potatoes, apples, cheese, and so on. Take turns
blindfolding family members to see if they can guess
what they are eating.

• *What's Changed?* Have each family member get a partner. Stare at each other for 30 seconds. Turn back to
back and change one item on yourself. You could un-
button a button, put your watch on the opposite hand
or untie your shoe. Face each other and see if you can
guess what your partner changed.

• *Help Humpty Dumpty Out.* Toss your sofa cushions and
pillows on a pile. Let your children act out the dramatic scene of "Humpty Dumpty had a great fall." As
they fall on the cushions, "All the King's horses and all
the King's men" can try to put Humpty together again.

• *Amaze Your Children.* This last idea will totally amaze
your children—amaze them in the sense that they
probably never expected their parents to do something
like this. Set a plate on the table and fill it with one-
quarter cup of water. Tell your family you just read
about an amazing scientific discovery about the chem-
ical make-up of hair. The study showed that chemicals
in some hair strands reacted with those in other hair
strands. You want to re-create the experiment; ask two
family members to each pluck one strand of hair from

his or her head. Place the hairs in the water. Make up some more scientific jargon, describing how pretty soon the two hairs will move toward each other and actually "fight" by twisting together. Be sure to stare intently at the two hairs. Say, "Look, they're starting to move together!" As your family bends over and gets closer and closer to the plate, quickly plop your hand in the middle of the plate, splashing everyone with water. The surprise element is so strong because everyone is focused on the two "fighting hairs."

Use these ideas as a springboard for creative ways to have fun with your family. It won't be long before you're qualified to write an article for a magazine that reads "122 Creative Family Activities"!

And If You Still Don't Believe that Fun Makes a Difference . . .

When our oldest daughter, Trina, was young, she loved playing Hide and Seek. At times we'd play a "normal" version and other times we announced, "Hide and Seek is scheduled for 7:30 tonight." That gave each of us time to prepare elaborate hiding places. My husband went so far as to construct a false wall in a closet so that we couldn't find him. During one game, I emptied a 50-pound bag of dog food so that Trina could hide inside it. As Trina lay quietly in the dog food bag, our 180-pound St. Bernard came by, noticed something different about his beloved dog food and plopped on top of the bag. It was definitely an unexpected variation on the game, but how we laughed about it!

Note
1. Maggie Scarf, *Intimate Worlds: Life Inside the Family* (New York: Ballantine Publishing, 1997), n.p.

11

Celebrating the Great Outdoors

We still do not know one thousandth of one percent
of what nature has revealed to us.

ALBERT EINSTEIN

When I participated in the *Trading Spouses* reality TV show,
I switched places for one week with a mom who seldom encouraged her family to take advantage of outdoor opportunities
available to them. One day, I insisted that my "new family" and
I go on a morning hike. Everyone grumbled—they were very open
about how much they disliked the idea of actually being outside and having to walk.

I ignored their protests, and we headed up a well-worn path
on a popular hiking trail. The 8- and 12-year-olds were soon so
tired that we had to rest frequently. They physically couldn't
keep up with this 53-year-old mom (and I'm not a fitness fanatic
by any means). The kids got so tired that the producer actually
cancelled the hike after 40 minutes, saying it wasn't safe to push
the kids so hard. I couldn't help but see the irony in the situation as two moms with preschoolers and babies in Snugglies casually walked by us while the producer explained his decision to
cancel the hike for these capable—but unwilling—young people.

We slowly walked down the trail. I decided to turn the experience into a nature stroll. We compared leaf shapes, looked for
bugs and tried to identify shoe brands from the sole imprints
in the dirt. (That last activity probably isn't described in nature
books, but it does involve dirt.) The kids showed an interest in

the leaves, bugs and dirt—it was all new to them.

As everyone got into the car, the dad said, "I never thought I'd say this, but I actually enjoyed that hike."

For adults and children used to spending most of their time indoors, a nature hike can be a new and exciting activity. But as evidenced by my *Trading Spouses* experience, making the switch from indoor to outdoor activities can't happen all at once.

Here are some ways to get started during the next month.

Silvana's Four-Week "Let's Get Started Celebrating the Great Outdoors" Program

Week One

Take the family to a park. Give each family one aspect of nature to observe. Your daughter might select leaves while your son volunteers to report on animal life. Mom or Dad could keep everyone updated on varieties of tree bark. As you walk, each person points out his or her topic of interest. The conversation might go like this:

"Look at that squirrel in the tree!"

"Here's the biggest leaf I've found so far!"

"Feel the bark on this Madrona tree. Isn't it smooth?"

Your whole family ends up gaining a new awareness of nature while getting exercise in the process.

Week Two

Plant something. And remember, your options for planting are limited only by the season and climate. If space is limited, grow herbs in a container on your windowsill or some flowers on the deck. You can even make a mini-garden by growing radishes in a plastic bag. Just make sure that all your containers have drain holes, 2 to 3 inches of gravel and good quality potting soil.

Growing prizewinning tomatoes is not the goal. Having children discover the miracle of seeing a tiny seed produce a pumpkin—that's what's important.

Week Three
Become amateur bird watchers. There's no need to travel to Mt. Haleakala on Maui to try to glimpse the po'ouli, considered one of the rarest birds in the world. You'll find plenty of bird activity in your own yard or at a local park.

If it's spring, supply the birds with a variety of items to build their nests. Collect small pieces of string, embroidery floss and hair from your hairbrush. Place these in the tree branches close to your house. A few weeks from now, you might see your leftover red craft yarn interwoven in a bird's nest.

Take the family to a specialty wild bird shop. Local store owners are a wealth of information and will deliver a passionate lecture about the importance of buying "proper" bird seed rather than generic brands from a discount store. Take their advice. Buy some high-quality seed and watch the birds flock to your house for their gourmet meals.

Week Four
On Monday, brainstorm a list of outdoor activities. Go ahead and get wild by suggesting a family trip to the Galapagos Islands. Accept everyone's suggestions, ranging from a walk though the neighborhood to using your family vacation to volunteer at a nature conservancy.

Having trouble coming up with ideas that everyone can agree on? See what the family thinks of these outdoor activities:

- Riding bikes
- Camping at a local state park (borrow camping equipment if you don't have any)

- Visiting a you-pick apple orchard or strawberry field
- Trying cross-country skiing or snowshoeing
- Wading in a creek
- Visiting an outdoor planetarium
- Helping the Parks and Recreation Department with a trail clean-up project

After you've made your list, pick one activity to do the next weekend. Then post the list in a conspicuous spot. When looking for an outdoor-related activity, use your customized list as an easy resource.

Congratulations! You've just completed another Four-Week Program on the great outdoors. See you at the campground!

Ask the Fun Consultant

Silvana, I understand that it's important to be outdoors, but I'm not a botanist or expert on bugs. I don't even like bugs! How can I help my children learn to enjoy nature?

You don't need to have a degree in Outdoorology. There are many ways to help your children learn to appreciate the world God made. Consider some of these ideas:

- In *The Sound of Music*, Maria takes the children tree climbing. Do your children know how to climb trees? They should! Overcome your fear of heights, and let children climb on trees with sturdy branches. You might get so inspired that you'll join Tree Climbers

International—check out www.treeclimbing.com. This organization actually has classes on tree climbing for both kids and adults (wearing outfits made from old bedroom drapes not required).

- How often do we tell children "Be careful, you'll fall"? Many children don't have the opportunity to run on grass, because most playgrounds are filled with wood chips or safety padding. But kids enjoy the simple freedom of running outside. Find a large grassy area and play traditional games such as Tag, Red Rover, Red Rover or Red Light, Green Light. If and when they fall down, the grass will catch them.

- Take a nature walk and look for unusual shapes. So often, children think that all trees have a solid brown trunk and leafy branches. As you walk, ask your children to look for twisted tree trunks or branches that look like a witch's fingernails. How many shapes of leaves can they discover? What are the different textures found on tree bark? As you walk, ask each child to find two or three small, unusual pieces of wood on the ground. Upon returning home, brush any dirt or moss off the pieces of wood, and then set out an assortment of paints and brushes. Watch children turn their pieces of wood into creative works of art. Maybe a narrow twig turns into a speckled snake. With the addition of paper wings, a smooth piece of wood could be transformed into a beautiful butterfly.

- Many children's museums and conservatories have butterfly gardens. It's amazing to see the look of wonder in a child's eyes when a butterfly lands lightly on his or her arm. With a little advance planning, you can create a butterfly garden at home. Choose a sunny, sheltered area to plant butterfly-attracting plants. But-terflies like large clumps of color, so plant flowers in bunches. Butterflies especially like nectar from asters, black-eyed susans, goldenrod and zinnias. Depending on the time of year, children can help plant, weed or simply observe the development of your butterfly gar-den. As kids work in the soil, encourage them to gently touch worms or caterpillars.

- Add interest to an ordinary hike with some of these variations: If you don't have nature trails, simply walk on city streets and turn the event into a coin walk. Let children take turns flipping a coin at every street cor-ner. Heads means you turn left, tails says you walk to the right. Who knows where you'll end up?

- Have preschoolers with you? Give each child a piece of colored paper. As you hike, see how many objects they can find to match their color. On other days, give young children paper cut into a particular shape, then help them identify real-life items that match their shape.

- Don't let a little rain stop you. An everyday walk takes on a new experience as children walk through mud puddles. Let children squish mud between their fin-gers. How about making a few mud pies?

Silvana, I'd like to do some of those activities with my kids, but they range in age from six months to six years. How can I do something outdoors that appeals to all of them?

How about a backyard camping trip? Your older children will enjoy the experience of sleeping outside in a tent, and you will still have the comforts of home for the baby. Invite another family to join in the festivities. That way, if you need to go indoors with an infant or toddler, other Fun-Filled Parents are available to monitor the outdoor activities.

After setting up the tent, bring out the sleeping bags. Add stuffed animals to enhance the fun. Ahead of time, get some library books about the great outdoors—your children will enjoy reading in their cozy tent. Then bring out the binoculars and look for birds or squirrels.

If making a fire isn't possible, go ahead and make s'mores on the barbeque. Children can still roast their marshmallows on the flame and squish the gooey mess between two graham crackers. The whole point is to get a sticky face and fingers.

As it gets dark, take a flashlight walk around the backyard. It's amazing how your ordinary yard takes on a different appearance as you view the bushes and trees with flashlights. Of course, don't forget to play Flashlight Tag! Establish a tree or picnic table as Base. Everyone hides, with flashlights off. The goal is to touch Base without getting "zapped" by the light from the flashlight belonging to "It."

Do you live in an area that has an abundance of fireflies? Give children clear plastic containers and try to catch a few. After a few minutes of observing the fireflies close up, release them so that they can twinkle for other campers.

See? You can have a nature activity right in your backyard—complete with the comforts of clean, indoor plumbing.

And If You Still Don't Believe that Fun Makes a Difference . . .

Living in the Seattle area meant that winter rain and wind storms were a common occurrence. One blustery evening, Sondra and I were reading and I casually asked Allan, "Is it still windy outside? I don't hear anything."

Allan walked out the back door, presumably to check on the weather. A few minutes later the door burst open and Allan yelled, "Yes, it's still windy!"

Glancing up, Sondra and I saw Wild-Tree-Man-on-a-Windy-Night. Using duct tape, he had attached tree branches to his head, his arms and legs. More branches were sticking out from inside his shirt sleeves. Wet leaves were plastered to his hair and face.

Some people listen to weather reports on TV—my husband turns himself into a giant weather prop!

12

Meals Are More Than Food

Talk to your children while they are eating.
What you say will stay even after you are gone away.

INDIAN PROVERB

One of my favorite movies when I was growing up was *Pollyanna*, starring Hayley Mills. Even though they weren't fashionable, I wore dresses with dropped waists and huge bows in my hair to look like the optimistic little blonde girl. In the movie, Pollyanna, who is recently an orphan, comes to live with her rich, strict and dour Aunt Polly. Dinners take place in a formal dining room with stilted conversation and maids who cast stern looks at Pollyanna to warn her away from spilling food on the linen tablecloth. Fun and frivolity were not part of the dining experience.

In the event your maids have the day off, why not use mealtime as another opportunity to have fun with your children? But before we get to the "fun" part of this chapter, let's look at some straight facts about family mealtime.

- According to a 2005 study by Columbia University, teenagers who eat with their families at least five times a week are more likely to get better grades and are much less likely to have substance abuse problems.[1]

- A University of Michigan study found that "mealtime is the single strongest predictor of better achievement and fewer behavioral problems. The importance of mealtime is far more powerful than time spent in school studying, sports and art activities."[2]

- Diane Beals, Ed.D., from the University of Tulsa, said, "A study of 80 preschoolers found that mealtime conversation built vocabulary better than listening to stories/reading out loud."[3]

- "The largest federally funded study of American teenagers found strong association between regular family meals (five or more per week with a parent) and academic success, psychological adjustment, and lower rates of alcohol/drug use, early sexual behavior, and suicidal risk."[4]

- A study of 4,746 adolescents in the Twin Cities area showed girls who ate five family meals a week were at about one-fourth the risk for extreme weight-control practices (such as anorexia and bulimia).[5]

Research and statistics may not be exciting to read, but the evidence shows that it's important for families to eat meals together. Of course, getting food on the table while rounding up family members is a difficult task. Luckily, this Four-Week Program is here to help. "Better a bread crust shared in love than a slab of prime rib served in hate" (Prov. 15:17, *THE MESSAGE*).

Silvana's Four-Week "Let's Get Started Eating Together" Program

Week One

At the beginning of the week, check everyone's schedule and find a minimum of two days when the family can eat together. Be creative. One family had parents with flexible work schedules, so they made a point of allowing 20 minutes for the family to eat breakfast together every morning. What a great way to start the day!

Week Two

Let the family know which days are designated as "Eat Together Day." Plan something special at these mealtimes. There's no need to serve expensive prime rib with imported truffles, but why not buy (or create) new placemats and eat by candlelight? Serve a unique vegetable or fruit such as jicama or star fruit. Read a funny article at the table. Switch places at the dinner table—let the youngest child sit in Dad's chair, Mom sits across from her usual place, and so on.

Week Three

Is it possible to add one more evening of eating together? Make this third evening special by eating in a different location. That's right—why be ordinary and eat at the kitchen table? Get brave and eat *under* the kitchen table. Or take your dinner and eat on the front steps, observing traffic in your neighborhood.

One family on a limited budget celebrated Friday Night Crazy Location Night. Each child took turns deciding where the family would eat around the house. One week the family ate in the attic. The following week found them sitting on the backyard swing set. Neighborhood children, hearing about the fun activity, soon started coming over on Friday, hoping to be asked to dinner.

Week Four

Are mealtimes enjoyable? Make sure to keep the atmosphere pleasant. That means you'll need to choose another time to harp on your daughter's messy room. And it definitely means resisting the temptation to nag about proper dining etiquette. Instead, if your child needs help with table manners, use a favorite technique at summer camps across the country: When a child has elbows on the table or forgets to use a napkin, he or she has to do a silly task such as skipping around the dining hall, singing, "Everyone should use a napkin, and everyone should use a napkin." If you don't have a massive dining hall, ask your child to skip around the dining table. You make your point about table manners without nagging.

You're probably excited about the idea of having all your loved ones around the table at mealtime. But perhaps you're wondering if the Four-Week Program is all you need. Here are some more ideas for how to make the time around the dinner table pleasant for everyone:

- To help family members focus on each other, turn off the TV and radio.

- Take turns saying grace before dinner. For variety, sometimes thank God *after* you've eaten the food.

- Don't worry about planning elaborate meals. The point of being together for dinner is the process of eating and sharing. Set out baked potatoes with a variety of toppings, and let family members serve themselves. Spend time being together instead of worrying whether or not the soufflé will flop.

- Assign children the rotating task of creating a table centerpiece and then explaining their choice during mealtime. One two-year-old carefully selected a smooth rock from the backyard and covered it with pieces of tape to "make it shiny." Naturally, Mom and Dad told her it was truly a one-of-a-kind centerpiece.

- Want to really impress your kids? Tell them about the "good ole days" when you (or your parents) pulled into a drive-up restaurant and waitresses on roller skates delivered meals to your car. Prepare a simple dinner and get everyone situated in the car. No need for seatbelts, because you're not going anywhere. Have an adult place boards across the car from window to window to create tables, and then eat your meal in the car. If you feel extra motivated, wear roller skates while serving your family!

• Pick a time to eat together other than dinner. One Saturday morning in December, my husband announced he would be making breakfast. Sondra and I didn't pay much attention until he said, "Breakfast's ready. Be sure to wear your coat and hats!" My creative husband had made a delicious breakfast of eggs, biscuits and hash browns—and then served it to us outside on the deck, in a breezy 36 degrees. Why not plan a picnic after church or a Saturday breakfast at the park?

• Bring out the fondue pot. If you don't have one, check any garage sale for a real bargain. Use the fondue pot to keep chocolate pudding warm. Dip in fruit chunks. Fondueing is a great way to slow down and enjoy conversation while having dessert.

• Enjoy even more family time around the dinner table by making indoor mini-s'mores. Set out an assortment of graham crackers, thin chocolate bars and miniature marshmallows. Break the graham crackers and chocolate bars into pieces about the size of a postage stamp. Here's the fun part: Instead of roasting marshmallows over a blazing fire, toast miniature marshmallows over a candle. Stick a toothpick in the marshmallow. Slowly hold one end of the toothpick over the candle flame, getting the marshmallow a golden brown. Place marshmallow between two graham crackers and chocolate. Then enjoy your bite-sized mini-s'more. (Children are usually very cautious when doing this, but if you worry about them burning themselves, use uncooked spaghetti instead of a toothpick.)

Ask the Fun Consultant

Silvana, I can get my family to eat together, but we really don't have "meaningful" conversation. Someone complains about their teacher, another child makes it clear he hates broccoli, and I end up giving ultimatums. Do you have some sort of "discussion starters" we can use so that we can get absorbed in something besides the dog's constipation problem?

Well, constipation (of the canine or conversational varieties) can be a problem! Take a look at these ideas for ways to get your children involved in an interesting conversation. Just remember to set guidelines so that family members show respect for the opinions of others. No one wants to be ridiculed because of an idea they share at the dinner table.

Ask family members to finish these sentences:

- When I'm older, I want to travel to . . .
- If I were principal at my school, I would . . .
- If my parents let me, I would . . . (This can be an eye-opener)
- If I had an extra $25, I would . . .
- I always laugh when . . .
- If I could be another person, I would be . . .
- If I could have any pet, I'd like to get . . .

Or try this: Find a colorful basket or jar, and fill it with strips of paper listing various questions or topics for discussion. Family members then take turns selecting the paper and answering the question. But remember, there's no pressure to stay on topic—if your child wants to pick another piece of paper, that's fine.

Some questions might be:

· What's your favorite animal and why?
· What is your favorite book?
· What's your favorite ride at the amusement park?
· What's the last thing you did to make someone laugh?
· What would your dream bedroom look like?
· Can you recite a Bible verse from memory?
· What's your favorite season and why?
· What famous person would you like to meet?
· Describe what it takes to be a good friend.

Whew! That's a lot of topics to discuss. If you still need more ideas to make mealtime meaningful, you can buy a card game called *Making Family Meals Fun Again* from www.uncommon goods.com. The kit offers activity cards designed to let you play games and have meaningful discussions with your family.

Those are great ideas for "going deep" with my family, Silvana, but do you have any ideas for keeping things light? We need to focus on having fun during mealtime.

If you want a little fun, try these ideas:

· Before dinner, secretly place a sticker under someone's chair. Halfway through the meal, see who is the lucky "winner." That person gets to choose a family game to play after the table is cleared.

- As you begin eating, set the timer for five minutes. When you hear the "ding," everyone takes his or her plate and moves one chair to the left. This simple activity always gets everyone laughing.

- On slips of paper, write silly phrases such as "sick polka-dotted caterpillar," "slimy bananas covered with grass seed" and "purple dogs and orange popsicles." Pick a phrase and have everyone in the family incorporate the words into a silly sentence.

- Instead of talking at the table, sing. Yes, sing "Pleeeeease passss the maaaashed potatooooooes."

- Designate a plain white tablecloth as the "Just Because" tablecloth. A few times a year, bring out the tablecloth and let family members draw a picture on it using permanent markers. (Be sure to have plastic or newspaper under the tablecloth to prevent the markers from bleeding through to your table.) It's fun to see the cloth get filled in with family artwork over the years.

Bon appetit!

And If You Still Don't Believe that Fun Makes a Difference . . .

Sometimes mealtimes should just be times to eat together without any "structured" activity. Last week we sat at the dinner table, lit the candles, said grace and began eating. Suddenly I said, "Oh, I forgot! I have this great article I want to read you from the *Wall Street Journal*." Quickly I raced upstairs, found the newspaper clipping and returned to an empty dinner table. Even the candles were gone. Hearing giggles, I found Allan and

Sondra holding their plates, eating in the laundry room. They dramatically pleaded with me not to share another enlightening article with them at dinner. I guess I can take a hint.

Notes

1. "Ten Reasons Why Family Dinners Are Important," University of Southern Maine Employee Wellness Program, referencing "10 Ways Teens Benefit from Family Dinners" at WebMD. http://www.usm.maine.edu/wellness/programs_and_serv ices/family_dinners.html (accessed February 2008).
2. Sandra L. Hofferth, "Changes in American Children's Time, 1981-1997," University of Michigan's Institute for Social Research, Center Survey, January 1999.
3. "Mealtime Conversations Help Kids Communicate—Study Shows that Language Skills of Preschoolers Are Enhanced If Parents Talk to Them During Meals," Society for the Advancement of Education, December 1995. http://findarticles.com/ p/articles/mi_m1272/is_n2607_v124/ai_17862972 (accessed February 2008).
4. William J. Doherty, PhD, "Overscheduled Kids, Underconnected Families: The Research Evidence," University of Minnesota Family Social Sciences Department. http://www.takebackyourfamilytime.umn.edu/downloads/research.pdf (accessed February 2008).
5. "Regular Family Meals Promote Healthy Eating Habits," *Science Daily*, November 18, 2004. http://www.sciencedaily.com/releases/2004/11/041116232104.htm (accessed February 2008).

13

Recipes You'll Never Want to Eat

Life loves to be taken by the lapel and told, "I'm with you kid. Let's go!"
MAYA ANGELOU

Watch any typical daytime talk show and you'll see hosts glee-fully whipping up tasty treats designed for parents and children to make together. The host explains the close-knit relationship you'll develop while making "Easy French Crepes" with your little Suzette. Yes, mothers and children are destined to have a lifetime of warm fuzzy feelings all due to the fact that they cooked or baked together.

I'm all for doing things with your children, but when it comes to cooking, I'm a failure. It makes no sense to me to spend time mixing and stirring ingredients that will be eaten in 15 minutes. Mix up a batch of homemade play dough, though, and you'll be investing in hours of fun with your children. (And think of all the calories you avoid by not eating mounds of raw cookie dough.)

When Sondra was seven, I read a memoir in which a woman extolled the joy she felt coming home from school to the smell of her mother's freshly baked cookies. That was when it hit me: I was a horrible mother! Sondra never arrived home to the smell of freshly baked cookies. But wait—I could make the *smell* without having to make the cookies.

Right before she came home from school, I boiled a pot of water on the stove, adding cinnamon and vanilla. Sure enough, Sondra walked in the door and said, "Wow! That smells good!"

I explained it was the smell of freshly baked cookies. "Cool," she answered. "Will you go on a bike ride with me?" Off we went. I felt reassured because my daughter had indeed come home to the smell of warm cookies, and we were building a warm fuzzy relationship by riding bikes together.

For all of you Fun-Filled Parents who (unlike me) like cooking with your children, get hold of some of these books:

- *Betty Crocker Kids Cook!* (Betty Crocker Publishing, 1999)
- *Everything Kid's Cookbook*, by Sandra Nissenberg (Adams Media, 2002)
- *Disney's Family Cookbook*, by Deanna Cook (Disney Publishing, 1996)

However, if you're looking for some non-edible and nontraditional recipes, you're reading the right book already. Why not begin with this Four-Week Program? What are you waiting for? Let's get started making those recipes you'll never want to eat (but will sure have fun making).

Silvana's Four-Week "Let's Get Started Making Some Recipes You'll Never Want to Eat" Program

Week One

Here's a way to make the house smell like fresh cookies without actually mixing flour, sugar, baking soda and eggs together to create edible cookie dough.

Cinnamon Applesauce Air Fresheners

Here's what you'll need:

1 cup applesauce (cheapest brand possible)
1½ cups cinnamon

⅓ cup glue
Cookie cutters
Waxed paper
Thin ribbon
Straw

Follow these steps:

1. Blend applesauce, cinnamon and glue until mixture forms a smooth ball. If too sticky, add more cinnamon.
2. Chill for about 30 minutes.
3. Roll dough on waxed paper, about ¼ to ½ inch thick.
4. Use cookie cutters to cut shapes.
5. Use the straw to make a hole in the top of each shape (for hanging).
6. Let dry at room temperature for 2 days.
7. String a ribbon through each hole, and hang "cookies" around the house for a warm, cozy smell.

These air fresheners also make great Christmas tree ornaments. Just use holiday cookie cutters for the shapes, and hang the cookies from your tree.

Week Two

You can buy play dough at the store, or you can show your children how to make this homemade version that smells delightful. They'll spend hours molding and shaping this pliable clay.

Smelly Play Dough (Good Smelly, that Is!)

Here's what you need:

1 cup flour
½ cup salt
3 tablespoons oil

1 packaged unsweetened powdered drink mix
¾ to 1 cup boiling water

Follow these steps:

1. Have children mix together flour, salt, oil and drink mix.
2. Have an adult slowly add boiling water, until mixture is the consistency of play dough.
3. Put dough on a kitchen counter top and knead to mix ingredients.
4. Let children poke, shape, prod, mold and play with dough.
5. Mixture stores well if placed in an airtight bag or container in refrigerator.

Week Three

You've probably seen brightly colored pasta in craft stores, but there's no need to pay top dollar when you can dye your own. Follow my secret (and cheap) recipe for colored pasta.

Rainbow Pasta

Here's what you need:

1 cup rubbing alcohol
Food coloring (use colors of your choice)
Uncooked pasta (large rigatoni are great for making colorful necklaces, while other dyed pasta shapes can be glued on paper or to each other to create colorful sculptures)

Follow these steps:

1. Add 4 to 5 drops of food color to 1 cup of rubbing alcohol.
2. Stir and add uncooked pasta.
3. Using a slotted spoon, remove the colored pasta and let drain on old newspapers. Pasta dries within a few hours.

4. Add more uncooked pasta to the leftover food coloring, until mixture is gone.

5. Repeat the process with other colors.

Week Four

Here's a recipe for pies that look and smell great. Just don't try to eat one!

Sweet, Smelly Mini-Pies

Here's what you need:

4 cups flour
1 cup salt
1½ cups hot water
Assortment of potpourri
Cookie sheet

Follow these steps:

1. Mix salt and hot water so that salt dissolves.
2. Add flour.
3. Mix until mixture is smooth.
4. Give kids chunks of dough and ask them to make mini-pie shells.
5. Fill each "pie" with a few dried fruits or flower petals.
6. Roll out excess dough into short strips.
7. Attach a few strips to top of pie to create a lattice effect.
8. Bake pies on cookie sheet for about 1 hour at 300 degrees.
9. Let cool before displaying.

Your children have learned all about measuring and mixing ingredients, just as if they were cooking "real" food. However, instead of making cookies that will soon get eaten, you now have long-lasting cinnamon air fresheners, homemade play dough and miniature pies. Let's not forget the colorful designer pasta necklace you can wear with your favorite evening gown (well, maybe wear it with your favorite nightgown).

Ask the Fun Consultant

Silvana, the last four weeks were some of my family's most fun ever in the kitchen. Can you share a few more inedible recipes?

Can I? You bet!

Chunky Bead Necklaces

Instead of buying expensive necklaces with fragile beads, have your children make you a necklace with these beads that make a very bold statement.

Here's what you need:

1 cup salt
½ cup cornstarch
½ cup boiling water
Saucepan
Toothpicks
Paint brushes with small bristles
Acrylic paint

Follow these steps:

1. Mix the salt and cornstarch in a saucepan.
2. Have an adult add ½ cup boiling water.
3. Stir well.

4. Keep mixture over low heat for 3 to 4 minutes.

5. Remove from heat.

6. To cool, turn out onto a smooth surface, such as a kitchen counter.

7. Have children form dough into bead shapes.

8. Use a toothpick to form a hole in the center of each bead.

9. Let beads dry overnight and then paint to create customized beads.

Slurch!

You'll have so much fun letting this gooey substance trickle through your fingers that you'll probably take it to work as a stress reliever.

Here's what you'll need:

1 tablespoon Mule Team Borax (available in the laundry detergent section of your grocery store)
8 ounces white school glue (Elmer's works best)
½ cup very hot but not boiling water
1 cup very cold water
A few drops food coloring if you desire

Follow these steps:

1. In a glass bowl, mix together cold water, white glue and food coloring.

2. Stir well.

3. In a separate bowl, dissolve the Borax powder in the very hot water.

4. Add Borax mixture to glue mix and stir. Mixture will seem clumpy and stretchy at the same time.

5. Remove the lump of Slurch and knead with your hands.

6. Within a few minutes, the substance will become a smooth mass that doesn't stick to your hands.

7. Amaze your children by telling them that Slurch is a non-Newtonian fluid—it is not liquid or solid, yet it has properties of both. (Isn't this better than baking ordinary cupcakes?)

8. If you can get kids to stop playing with the Slurch, store in the refrigerator in a sealed container.

Homemade Silly Putty

Why buy Silly Putty at the store when your children can make a big batch at home?

Here's what you'll need:

½ cup Sta Flo Liquid Starch
½ cup Elmer's Glue
A few drops food coloring (if you want colored Silly Putty)

Follow these steps:

1. Mix the glue, food coloring and starch together with a spoon.

2. After the mixture is stirred, knead it with your hands until it turns to the consistency of Silly Putty.

3. Store in the refrigerator in an airtight container.

Bubble Paints

This is one of my personal favorites.

Here's what you'll need (for each color):

2 teaspoons dishwashing liquid
½ cup water

2 tablespoons powdered tempera (available at craft or office
      supply stores in the paint aisle)
Drinking straw
Jar with lid

Follow these steps:

1. Blend the dishwashing liquid, water and powdered
   tempera in a lidded jar. To deepen the color, add
   more tempera.
2. Set the jar on newspaper to protect the work surface.
   Gently blow through the straw into the paint mixture. *Do not* suck in—the mixture tastes terrible and
   might make you sick. Keep blowing until the bubbles overflow.
3. To create a bubble print, remove the jar and gently
   place a piece of paper on top of the overflow of bubbles. They will leave a print on the paper before and
   after they burst. Lay the paper flat to dry.

Finger Paints

If you're thinking that your kids are too old for this one, think
again. If *you* get in on the action, kids of any age will have tons
of fun with finger painting.

Here's what you need:

4 tablespoons sugar
½ cup cornstarch
2 cups cold water
Few drops of dish detergent
Assorted colors of food coloring
3 or 4 small bowls

Shiny-sided paper, such as freezer paper (available at your grocery store or butcher shop) or finger paint paper

Follow these steps:

1. Mix sugar and cornstarch together in a medium saucepan. Under adult supervision, stir in the 2 cups water. Keep stirring and cook over medium heat until mixture comes to a boil.
2. Boil for 4 to 5 minutes so that mixture can thicken.
3. Remove from heat and allow to cool.
4. Divide the mixture into 3 or 4 small bowls. Add a drop of food color and a drop of detergent to each bowl, creating different colors of finger paint.
5. Mix well, then let children paint, using their fingers as brushes. For best results, paint on freezer paper or purchased finger paint paper.

Face Paints

Your children probably enjoy getting their face painted at family festivals or carnivals. Now they can do it themselves.

Here's what you need:

2 tablespoons shortening
1 tablespoon cornstarch
3 or 4 small bowls
3 or 4 drops food coloring
Small makeup sponges, paintbrushes or cotton swabs

Follow these steps:

1. Mix shortening and cornstarch in a bowl until smooth.
2. Divide mixture into 3 or 4 bowls.

3. Add a different food coloring to each bowl and mix well.
4. Paint your face using the brushes or cotton swabs.
5. If you feel ambitious, set up a face-painting booth at the next community festival.

Chunky Sidewalk Chalk

Your children will be amazed at how they can make their own chalk with just a few simple ingredients.

Here's what you need:

2 cups loosely packed Plaster of Paris (can be purchased at any craft or hardware store)
1 cup water
Liquid or powdered tempera paint
Empty margarine or yogurt containers
Disposable molds, such as toilet-roll tubes or Styrofoam egg cartons
Squirt of dishwashing liquid

Follow these steps:

1. Pour Plaster of Paris into a container.
2. Using a disposable stick, stir in most of the water until the mixture is the consistency of thick pudding. If mixture is too thick, add 1 to 2 teaspoons of water.
3. Add 2 to 3 tablespoons of paint and mix well.
4. Drop thick mixture into the molds. If using toilet-paper rolls, wrap aluminum foil around one end so mixture doesn't leak out.
5. Let mixture stand for 1½ to 2 hours or until fairly firm.
6. Gently remove from molds and let dry overnight before drawing colorful designs on your sidewalk.

Big Blue Bubbles

Who doesn't love blowing bubbles and then popping them in midair? Here's a recipe designed to produce some *really* big bubbles. Try blowing a bubble, catching it and putting it in the freezer. For even more fun, blow bubbles at night and see how they shimmer when you shine a flashlight on them.

Here's what you need:

1 cup water
2 tablespoons light Karo syrup or glycerin (glycerin can be found in drug stores)
4 tablespoons Joy dishwashing liquid

Follow these steps:

1. Mix together water, syrup or glycerin, and dishwashing soap.
2. Let set 24 hours for best results (that is, for the biggest bubbles).
3. Blow and start popping!

I hope that reading through these recipes has gotten you excited about spending time with your kids. Happy cooking!

And If You Still Don't Believe that Fun Makes a Difference . . .

Because I'm not fond of cooking, I look for ways to incorporate store-bought foods into "activities." A few weeks ago I bought a package of fortune cookies and painstakingly removed the fortunes with tweezers. Then I wrote my own fortunes on tiny strips of paper and poked them back into the cookies. Knowing Sondra ate lunch with her soccer team, I suggested she share the cookies with the team. Her friends were shocked to read fortunes that said things like, "You will score many goals at the soccer game tomorrow" and "Grass stains will soon cover your gold and purple soccer uniform." They couldn't figure out how all the fortunes applied to them. (Although one girl did get suspicious and ask, "Since when are the fortunes in these things written by hand?")

14

Volunteering: A Family Activity

When you are kind to others, it not only changes your life,
it changes the world.

HAROLD KUSHNER

At one time or another, every parent across the country has groaned in despair, "How did I raise such self-centered children? All they think about is, *What's in it for me?* Why don't they appreciate what a good life they have? If only they knew how I had to walk to school in the snow with holes in my shoes and no winter coat, without eating breakfast after feeding the pigs at five in the morning, chased to school by a gang of bullies!"

After you compose yourself, you probably come up with the next major proclamation: "This family is going to start volunteering. Yes, we're going to help other people so that my kids can see what a wonderful life they have." Reality sets in and you soon decide that volunteering to serve soup at a homeless shelter in a "shady" part of town may not be feasible with your six- and eight-year-old children.

Now what?

First of all, take a deep breath and relax. All children have a tendency to feel that the world revolves around them. As parents, we can find ways to broaden our children's horizons and teach them empathy. Ken Bentley, administrator of the Nestle Very Best in Youth Program, says, "By volunteering, young people experience the many blessings that come with giving service to others. They also learn important life skills like being responsible, organization, leadership and a caring spirit."[1]

The following are four valuable lessons children learn as a result of volunteering.

1. Children learn that they are not the center of the universe

How often have your children said, "Mom, you know I don't like crusts on my sandwich"? Or how about this one: "But I don't want to help Grandma clean her garage." And I know you've heard this: "Why do I have to wait until these jeans go on sale?"

When children volunteer, they see beyond their safe world of family, school and sports. They gain an awareness of people or animals that need assistance. Visiting the elderly in a nursing home or seeing abandoned cats at the Humane Society gives children some perspective on their lives—and the world.

In 2001, 10-year-old Anthony Leanna visited his grandmother in the hospital. His comfortable world was disturbed by seeing people in the cancer unit losing their hair. How did he react? Anthony began Heavenly Hats, a program that collects new hats to donate to cancer patients. Today Anthony is 15 and spends about 10 hours a week collecting, sorting and packaging hats. "I just want to put a smile on people's faces," he said. "That's the point of the whole program."[2] His website, www.heavenly hats.com, describes the program and provides guidelines for donating hats.

2. Children learn responsibility and gain self-confidence

When children volunteer, they often find themselves in a position in which responsibility is required. Did they sign up to plant flowers at the community center? Then it's important that they arrive at the designated time and location. As children volunteer, they discover a newfound sense of being needed, and they gain self-confidence when they know they've made a real contribution to a volunteer project. The Search Institute reports that youth who volunteer just one hour a week are 50 percent less likely to abuse drugs, alcohol and cigarettes or to engage in destructive behavior.[3] So get your children involved in volunteering.

3. Children learn about community resources

Spend time with your child discussing various volunteer possibilities. Does he or she want to get involved working with animals, the environment or people? Visit local programs to expose children to community groups that depend on volunteer efforts. You'll find opportunities to read books for the blind, collect gloves for the homeless or peel potatoes for a soup kitchen. One family heard the Humane Society needed toys for the animals. After a brainstorming session about community resources, they called the local tennis club to ask for donations of old tennis balls. The club was more than happy to donate their tired tennis balls on a regular basis.

When Sondra was 11, she was asked to be a spokesperson for Childcare Worldwide, a Christian relief agency based in our hometown of Bellingham, Washington. We didn't even know the local agency existed, and then suddenly we found ourselves visiting their children's homes in Kenya and Uganda. Later we saw their feeding program in Peru, which provides breakfast for 12,000 children on a daily basis. Today, at 18, Sondra speaks at conferences and schools around the country, stressing the importance of volunteering. Her book *77 Creative Ways Kids Can Serve* (Wesleyan Publishing) gives kids step-by-step directions on how they can take part in volunteer projects.

4. Children develop relationships with positive role models

We all want our children to have positive role models. As children work side by side with adults on volunteer projects, they observe adults giving time and effort to humanitarian causes. Instead of looking up to a rock star who advocates an "It's all about me" mentality, your children just might say, "Mom, Mr. Stevens is so cool! Do you know he helps sick eagles and hawks at the bird sanctuary? Can I go help him sometime?" Sound like something you'd like your child to say? Then you know what to do.

Do these four amazing outcomes encourage you to get your children involved in volunteer work? Maybe you and your kids have already gotten hooked on that amazing feeling that comes when we step out of ourselves and into service to others. Or maybe you're ready and willing but are still short on ideas for how your family could volunteer. If so, read on.

Silvana's Four-Week "Let's Get Started Volunteering" Program

Week One
What can you do to help? Explain to your children the importance of helping others, then ask them for ideas for how they think your family could be of service to your neighbor. Yes, your kindergartner will probably suggest something like taking poor kids to Disneyland. Keep that in mind as a possibility for a later date. In the meantime, brainstorm some more-attainable ideas.

If you get stuck and are short on ideas, see if any of the following interest your family:

- Collect hotel-sized shampoos and soaps for "We Care" kits to donate to homeless shelters.
- Ask recreation centers if they'll save their old tennis balls. Then take them to animal shelters.

- Collect newspaper to give to dog shelters for puppy cages.
- With your family, volunteer as dog walkers at a local animal shelter.
- Start being a pen pal with a missionary's child overseas.
- Make no-sew fleece blankets.
- Start a butterfly garden at a senior center or at a community park.
- Help the Parks and Recreation department with a clean-up project.
- Buy Forget-Me-Not seeds and send them to friends.
- Do a secret good deed for a neighbor, like cutting his or her grass and pulling weeds.
- Ask your friends to donate school supplies for underprivileged kids.
- Sort through your clothes and toys; donate whatever you no longer wear/play with to a worthwhile charity, such as the Salvation Army.
- Ask your family to sponsor a child through a Christian relief agency.
- If you have long hair, get it cut and donate it to Locks of Love (www.locksoflove.org).
- Collect donations of markers and cute bulletin board decorations for a new teacher.
- Offer to help a Sunday School teacher prepare for a craft activity or decorate her classroom.
- Cut out coupons from the newspaper and donate them to a nonprofit agency.

Week Two

Keep talking about ways the family can volunteer and try a simple at-home project.

Some researchers with too much time on their hands came up with this statistic: The average woman in America has 30 pairs of *extra* shoes in her closet! How about going through your closets and collecting gently worn shoes to donate to Soles4Souls? This amazing nonprofit agency distributes one pair of shoes every 28 seconds. Their goal is to impact the lives of as many people as possible through the gift of shoes. Casually ask friends and relatives to donate shoes. You'll be amazed at the shoes you'll collect. After you've collected the shoes, simply pack them in sturdy boxes and ship to a Soles4Souls warehouse in Alabama or Nevada, whichever is closest.

Soles4Souls, Inc.	Soles4Souls, Inc.
315 Airport Road	Foreign Trade Zone #89
Roanoke, AL 36274	6620 Escondido Street
	Las Vegas, Nevada 89119

They will sort the shoes and ship them to orphanages, flood or disaster victims, and other needy people around the world. So far, 3 million shoes have been sent to Russia, Romania, Africa, Guatemala and locations around the U.S. Get more details at www.soles4souls.org.

Week Three

As a family, choose a volunteer project that involves more than collecting a few clothes, toys and shoes. Use this week to plan your project for next week, which should involve more people than just your family. Begin with a manageable idea such as collecting dog food for a pet food bank. Consider asking neighbors to donate any extra pet food or talk to the manager of a local grocery store. Or maybe you'll plan on putting together a few Birthday Cake Kits for a women's shelter, complete with cake mixes, frosting and candles. Be sure to take the whole family along when you deliver the kits.

If you're still having difficulty coming up with an idea the whole family can be excited about, call a community volunteer agency for ideas. They match individuals looking for volunteers with agencies needing volunteers. One family found themselves helping at Special Olympic track meets; even the eight-year-old got involved by teaching a Special Olympic athlete to stay in his lane when running around the track.

Do you need to collect supplies or material? Will you have to coordinate with an agency? Start revving up some enthusiasm for the project with your family. Give children as much "ownership" of the project as possible.

Week Four

This is it! Your first family volunteer project! Take pictures of family members working together. A few days after completing the project, discuss the event. Was it too complicated? Could everyone in the family participate? Decide whether you want to do the same project again or if you are ready to move on to more-involved projects. Congratulate yourselves on a job well done.

Ask the Fun Consultant

Silvana, last week our pastor spoke about the importance of helping others. He spoke from James 1:27: "This is pure and undefiled religion in the sight of our God and Father, to visit orphans and widows in their distress and keep oneself unstained by the world." To be truthful, I don't know any orphans or widows who are in distress. What are some other ways I can get my family involved in volunteering? Is it possible to volunteer without having to drive kids all over town?

Of course it's possible! Now that you've completed one project, the world of volunteering is wide open to your family. Here are some more family-friendly volunteer opportunities that require varying levels of time, planning, financial investment—and driving.

- *Reading Fun.* Check to see whether the local library needs help with reading programs. Children can make posters about upcoming events or dress up as a storybook character while adults read stories.

- *Helping at Home.* Mother Teresa helped the poorest of the poor in India. People often wanted to move to India and help her. She told them that "Love begins at home, and it is not how much we do, but how much love we put in that action." She told people to stay home and volunteer in their own communities. Read a few books about Christian missionaries to inspire your family and to reinforce the gospel message that God *really* wants us to help others. With your family, make a list of ways you can volunteer throughout the year by collecting food for a food bank, organizing a coat drive for children of low-income parents, or walking dogs at the Humane Society.

- *Bedtime Snack Sacks.* Do your children enjoy a bedtime snack? What about homeless children or those living in shelters? Provide the family with an assortment of lunch sacks. Assign tasks to different family members. Some people can decorate the bags with glitter, stickers and funny drawings. Find small toys to include in each bag, along with a nonperishable granola bar and juice pack. Deliver the sacks to a shelter so that other children can enjoy a bedtime treat.

- *Secret Bulletin Board.* Make arrangements to go to your church and decorate a bulletin board in honor of your pastor. Have children draw borders and colorful pictures. Add balloons around the edges and make a heading that says, "Pastor So-and-So Is the Best!" If possible, get pictures of the pastor as a baby or graduating from seminary. Include space for other church members to write positive comments about the pastor.

· *Loose-Change Hunt.* Scour the house to collect as much loose change as possible. Check coat pockets, under seat cushions and in the car ashtray. Donate the money to a worthy cause. You might even simply buy a book of stamps and give it to a senior center to help a low-income senior pay the bills or stay in touch with his or her family and friends.

· *One-Day Project.* When November 18 rolls around, celebrate National Family Volunteer Day with a special one-day project.

· *Time to Perform.* Do your children have dramatic or musical talents? Encourage them to practice and present a "talent show" to a local nursing home. Invite some friends to add to the talent roster.

· *Sponsor a Child.* Can you sponsor a child in a developing country? Childcare Worldwide has sponsorship opportunities in Africa, India, Mexico and the Philippines. The organization spends only 4 percent of its budget on administrative costs. You can be assured your specific child gets the care that sponsorship provides. Check out www.childcareworldwide.org.

· *Buy My Daughter's Book!* As I mentioned, Sondra recently published a book called *77 Creative Ways Kids Can Serve* (Wesleyan Publishing, 2008) that gives step-by-step directions on how kids can get involved doing 77 different volunteer projects. It's easy to find a project that appeals to your child's age and interests.

I hope that all these ideas will get your family excited about how they can make a difference in your community. As you can see, volunteering means much more than serving soup at a soup kitchen. Your family will gain a sense of purpose and compassion as they reach out to help others.

Happy volunteering!

And If You Still Don't Believe that Fun Makes a Difference . . .

Not every volunteer project will turn out the way you expect. One year, we agreed to perform at a Christmas party for 300 underprivileged kids. Allan and I were experienced at doing magic shows and puppet shows for hundreds of groups, so we had looked forward to the event. But this group was tough! They screamed through the whole puppet show, even after the puppets "disappeared." They rushed Allan as he performed onstage and tried to grab his props. Then the youth leaders attempted to get the group quiet so that Santa could arrive, but the kids kept running around and yelling. Santa, who was 78 years old, got too hot waiting and fainted behind the puppet stage!

Another time, our family signed up to serve Easter dinner at a shelter. When we arrived, the director said he had more than enough volunteers (a good problem to have). He asked if we'd come back in three hours and help with cleanup. That was the year the Clark family spent Easter afternoon scrubbing toilets, mopping floors and washing countless pots and pans. It wasn't exactly what we had in mind, but we were able to meet a need and make a difference. We were reminded that it's not all about us—it's all about what God can do through us.

Similar experiences can teach your children valuable lessons. Sometimes we expect people to be eternally grateful for our "help." But Jesus tells us to serve others—He never says we will be awarded "Volunteer Family of the Year." Our job is to be obedient to Him, even though other people may not acknowledge us or our efforts. And the benefits of volunteering far outweigh any disappointment or occasional negative experience we might have.

Notes
1. Ken Bentley, from his address at the Nestle Very Best in Youth Award ceremony, June 2003.
2. Anthony Leanna, from a survey by the author in 2003.
3. Search Institute Developmental Assets, 1995. http://www.search-institute.org (accessed November 2006).

15

Creating Family Traditions

To be in your child's memories, you must be in their lives today.
ANONYMOUS

On an episode of *Everybody Loves Raymond*, Raymond's long-suffering wife, Deborah, decides to do something new for Thanksgiving. She decides that, instead of serving turkey, she'll make . . . fish. Yes—a plump, whole trout, lovingly displayed with lemon slices and sprigs of parsley. Naturally, the family is in an uproar when they see a fish instead of a turkey on the serving platter. *How can she serve fish?!* You *have* to have turkey on Thanksgiving. It's tradition!

In our busy society, traditions are a chance for families to connect emotionally, physically and spiritually. There's a certain comfort in knowing that Dad always makes pancakes on Saturday mornings or that Mom gives pedicures to the twins every Wednesday afternoon. Families feel connected on Sunday night when they read a Bible story by candlelight.

Some traditions involve hours of preparation, such as an annual family reunion with relatives from across the country. Other traditions can be as simple as driving around looking at Christmas lights wearing pajamas (Mom and Dad should wear sweatsuits in order to be decent in the event of an accident). What's important is the sense of "this is what our family does" on a regular basis.

Is your family a bit short on traditions, likely because you're always a bit short on time? How about beginning a Four-Week "Let's Get Started Making Traditions" Program?

Silvana's Four-Week
"Let's Get Started Making Traditions" Program

Week One

Get the family together and serve a fun snack such as root beer floats or different flavors of popcorn. Ask your children about the traditions your family has. You might be surprised to hear that they consider wrestling with Dad when he gets home from work to be a family tradition. After you've made your list, brainstorm some ideas for new traditions that can be done any time of the year. Here are some possibilities:

- Celebrate the first day of each month with an indoor or outdoor picnic.
- Put green food coloring in milk and serve it on St. Patrick's Day.
- Plan a "Take Down the Christmas Tree" party with lively music and special treats.
- Whenever you call Grandpa, always start by singing "For He's a Jolly Good Fellow."
- Greet your kids with balloons after their first day of school.
- Always make pancakes in the shape of bananas. No round pancakes allowed!

Week Two

Actually carry out one of the new traditions you discussed last week. Decide how often this new family event will take place.

Week Three

Find a way to connect with an older relative, either in person or by speaker-phone. Ask what traditions he or she remembers from childhood. Does your family observe some of those traditions? Pick one of your relative's holiday traditions and plan to celebrate it the next time the holiday comes around.

Week Four

Just for fun, meet with your family at the beginning of the week. Let your children plan a new surprise family tradition. If possible, allocate a small budget so that they can purchase supplies. Later in the week, celebrate the new tradition. Letting your child create a tradition gives him or her valuable skills in goal setting and following through on ideas. In addition, you'll end up with a family tradition celebrated by no other family.

So, was that more fun than you thought it could be? I bet you're well on your way now to being the new champions of traditions.

Ask the Fun Consultant

Silvana, my kids get really excited about birthdays. What traditions can we start to help them make their birthdays more memorable celebrations?

Yes, children love their birthdays. (Adults, on the other hand, would love to ignore their passing years.) Here are some easy ways to establish birthday-related traditions. (Remember, you don't have to do every one of these. Pick and choose what works for you.)

- Some families have a tradition of putting a dab of butter on the sleeping birthday person's nose. This is to guarantee "a smooth way for next year."

- Have family members hold candles (or flashlights if you don't want to burn the house down) and wake up the birthday child with a rousing chorus of "Happy Birthday."

- Before your son or daughter wakes up, sneak into their room and put up a few streamers and balloons. The decorations are an instant visual reminder to your child that "today is *your* special day."

- Foster a love of books by purchasing a "coffee table" book for your child on every birthday. The glossy photos and large size make an impact, especially compared to the usual low-cost books we purchase. In addition, older children will have a history of their interests as documented by the subject of each year's book.

- Younger children enjoy having parents eat lunch with them at school on their birthday. Warning: Do not show up at your 13-year-old's cafeteria with a pointed party hat and Mickey Mouse cupcakes. Your kindergartner, on the other hand, will declare you "the best dad in the universe!"

- Gather pictures of your child from the past year, specifically ones that show him or her doing various activities. Then glue the pictures onto a piece of cardboard. Write the year in the corner, and cover the cardboard with clear adhesive paper to create a birthday placemat. Children enjoying looking at past placemats, and seeing how they have grown and how their abilities have developed.

- At the end of the day, after the birthday festivities have ended, give your child a letter or poem you have written about him or her. Include specific reasons why he or she is special, and Bible verses that have meaning for you. Wrap up the letter by explaining why you are so glad to be your child's parent.

- Give the birthday child the gift of decision-making on his or her day. Eating ice cream for breakfast, wearing faded-but-loved jeans to school and selecting a birthday menu help create the sense that this really is your child's special day. (If your child wants to take his or her entire third-grade class out for lobster, you might want to discuss the concept of reasonable expectations.)

- With a flourish, announce that the birthday child is relieved from doing any chores today. Now that's a great no-cost present!

A fact to amaze your children: In Ireland, it is a birthday tradition to hold the child upside down by the ankles and give them "Birthday Bumps" on the head equal to the number of years they are. (I wonder how they do this for 16-year-old boys?)

That takes care of birthdays, Silvana. But what about other holidays?

Never fear—here are some simple ideas. Read on.

Valentine's Day
Here are a few ideas for Valentine's Day:

- You know that no one actually eats those rock-hard candy hearts, so buy a few boxes and announce a Heart Hunt instead. Hide the candy throughout the house, sticking them in nooks and crannies. Your children will love racing through the house, practicing for the upcoming Easter egg hunt. Don't worry if your kids don't find all the hearts. They'll show up throughout the year and bring you memories of love and kindness.

- Go wild with your heart-shaped cookie cutter. Make heart pancakes. Cut sandwiches into heart shapes. Make rice for dinner and pack the rice in the cookie cutter—tap the mold on the plate and you have heart-shaped rice. Make dough and create a home-made heart-shaped pizza. And here's a novel idea: Use the cookie cutter to make heart-shaped cookies.

- Announce to your family that you're setting up a kissing booth. (You'll get some groans, but with any luck, some takers too.) Set up an official kissing booth by cutting the bottom out of a large box and setting it on a table. Decorate the box. Sit behind it (pretending that you're on TV), and invite family members to approach you. Ask them a trivia question. If they answer correctly, they get a kiss—a real kiss or a chocolate kiss (your call).

Enough of hearts and flowers and mushy stuff. Let's get on to another holiday.

Surefire April Fool's Tricks

Somehow as adults get older, somewhat wiser and certainly somewhat heavier, April Fool's loses its appeal. Children, on the other hand, delight in announcing, "Look, Mom . . . it's snowing! April fool!" before you have a chance to act utterly surprised. With young children, be prepared to get tricked over and over—with the same gag, of course. This year get into the April Fool's spirit and start some of these traditions yourself.

- It's an old favorite, but it never fails to elicit great screams. Purchase plastic spiders or ants and put them in an ice cube tray. Add water, freeze and then serve cool, refreshing (and creepy-crawly) drinks to your unsuspecting family.

• Divide your family into two groups, making sure that each group has a good mix of ages and abilities (in other words, don't put the first- and third-graders in one group and Dad and your teen in another). Set the kitchen timer for 15 minutes, and secretly work on a trick to play on the other group of family members. Regroup after the allotted time and resume normal activities. Half the fun is wondering when and where the trick will take place.

• Remember when you had a Mystery Utensil Night at camp? Bring the tradition back to your own home. Right before dinner, place an assortment of kitchen utensils such as spatulas, large wooden spoons, ice cream scoops and potato mashers in a box. Before your family sits down for a pleasant meal, they must reach into the box without looking and remove a utensil. The chosen item is their only form of silverware. Have plenty of napkins handy.

Are you laughing yet? I hope so. And I hope that you will get into the spirit of the next April Fool's Day. Remember, there's nothing like enjoying laughter with the ones you love!

Low-Sugar, High-Fun Easter Basket Fillers

Tired of tricks? How about starting a tradition of having unusual Easter baskets? You can fill those Easter baskets with something besides chocolate and marshmallow Peeps—and still have your kids be happy with what the Easter Bunny brought.

Consider the interests of each individual family member and provide "theme baskets" as a new tradition.

- *Picasso Basket.* Budding artists enjoy receiving a new set of markers, specialty glues and stickers. Add a few cardboard frames so that they can display their future masterpieces.

- *Fix-It Basket.* Do you have a child who loves to see how things work? Check the Dollar Store for a basic set of screwdrivers and wrenches. Add a discarded radio or telephone, and you have just given your child the gift of discovery.

- *Baking Basket.* Give your child his or her own set of measuring spoons, sprinkles, cookie cutters and a kid-friendly cookbook.

- *Book Kit.* The bookworm in your family will enjoy a magazine subscription as well as a new book. Toss in a few bookmarks, as well as a pen and notebook to encourage his or her creative writing. Does your child need a new Bible? Easter is the ideal time for this gift.

- *Authentic Grass.* If you are organized enough to plan a few weeks ahead, line your children's Easter baskets with plastic. Add soil and

> ## Speaking of Peeps
>
> *Here are important things to know in case you suddenly are faced with Peep trivia questions:*
>
> When Peeps were first made in 1953, each individual Peep was squeezed out of a pastry bag. Each eye was hand-painted.
>
> The manufacturer produces 2 million Peeps daily.
>
> Check out their website at www.marshmallow peeps.com for craft and recipe ideas. We have a tradition of putting the cute little yellow Peeps in the microwave to watch them expand and turn into yellow ooze (not all traditions have to be deeply meaningful).

grass seed and keep moist. With enough spring sun-shine, your baskets should sprout full of grass in which to nestle their treats.

- *Bubble Bath and Beyond.* If you have preteen girls, they may feel that Easter baskets are too childish for their sophisticated lifestyle. Keep them happy by filling a wicker basket with decorative soaps, shampoos and body lotions. Don't forget to add nail polish and styling mousse. Add a gift card from a local Christian bookstore.

(*Warning:* These ideas are not substitutes for the traditional candies found in "normal" Easter baskets. They do, however, show your children how to be creative and open to new ideas.)

To combine the fun of family traditions with serving together, see if a member of your church will be alone at Easter. Consider getting together as a family and assembling a special basket for a shut-in or another adult who has no family living nearby. This person will delight in receiving an unexpected gift, and your family benefits from a tradition that helps other people.

Put the "Thanks" Back in Thanksgiving

The word "thanksgiving" evokes thoughts of delicious food rather than an appreciation for all we have. Children today take their lives for granted. Doesn't everyone have a computer? Don't all kids own several pair of shoes? Rather than telling children they don't know how good they have it (after all, you walked seven miles barefoot to school), try developing new family traditions that foster a sense of gratitude and thankfulness.

- *Thankful Candle.* Begin a year-round tradition with a Thankful Candle. Purchase a large candle and keep it in a special place. Whenever someone wants to share something he or she is thankful for, the candle is lit during dinnertime. Read Scripture verses based on the theme of giving thanks to God.

- *Sharing Goodies.* When baking for Thanksgiving, have children help bake a few extras. Wrap up your goodies and deliver them to a fire or police station as a way to thank community helpers.

- *Feeding Others.* Many books suggest volunteering to serve dinner at a shelter or mission on Thanksgiving. Often this is impractical with out-of-town guests or toddlers in the family. Instead, pick a time before Thanksgiving and ask a shelter what you can do at home to help. One shelter gave a family 50 pounds of potatoes to peel them at home.

- *Basket of Blessings.* As you set the table, place two kernels of dried corn next to everyone's plate. After the meal, pass around a small basket. Each person drops his or her kernels into the basket and mentions two things he or she is thankful for. Label the basket "Our Basket of Blessings," and keep in a prominent location as a reminder of God's blessings on your family.

- *The Special Plate.* Many families have a tradition called The Special Plate. As a family, go to a thrift shop or antique store and buy a plate that is different from your everyday dishes. (One family fell in love with a plate that depicted a rooster wearing roller skates!) Display the plate in a prominent location so that you won't forget to use it. Any time there's a special celebration that honors a particular family member, that person eats off the special plate. When Mom gets a promotion or Steve wins the class spelling bee, it's time to bring out the special plate. (I know a family who even had Grandpa eat off the special plate when he got new dentures.) For a more traditional approach, you can purchase "The Red Plate." This is a trademarked bright red plate that reads "You are special today" around the edges. It's available through Hallmark stores or online at www.catholicfamilygifts.com.

Maybe you're thinking, *I don't think my family really cares about traditions.* Just try serving a fish next Thanksgiving and see what they have to say!

A Memorable Christmas

You probably have more than enough traditions to go with Christmas, so I'm not going to share any new ideas with you. Okay, well . . . maybe just one—though it's not one you probably want to try.

One year we did something that I thought could be a meaningful Christmas tradition. Little did I know we would later try to erase the memory from our minds forever.

One holiday season, a particular headline in the newspaper caught my eye: "King Mountain Church Offers Walk Through Bethlehem." The article described an amazing free experience in which the public could stroll through a re-creation of ancient Bethlehem, complete with real camels, sheep, hundreds of authentically dressed characters and even a live Baby Jesus. Families were encouraged to visit and walk through a typical village similar to the one Mary and Joseph saw when they arrived in Bethlehem. The village featured food stalls, a sandal-making shop and, of course, a stable with a real baby. Since this was a yearly event, we decided to go and begin a new family tradition.

We realized how popular the program was when we discovered cars backed up on the road leading to the parking lot.

"Shepherds," complete with beards and long flowing robes, greeted us at the entrance. The first one said, "Bethlehem is pretty crowded tonight. I'm going to have you be the first to park in the overflow parking lot. Follow this road up the hill, and another shepherd will guide you to the remote parking area."

We dutifully followed directions and, sure enough, we met another shepherd (holding an adorable lamb) who told us, "Follow this road to the second left. Then turn right at the edge of the grove of trees. Take a sharp left after that turn and park there."

As we pulled away, my husband asked if I had understood the directions. "Of course!" I said, "We'll be the leaders to the remote parking area."

In the distance we could see Bethlehem, lit by torches. "That man's leading a camel!" shouted Sondra. I assured her we'd soon be walking through Bethlehem, up close and personal with the camel.

"This is the second left. Turn here," I instructed my husband. "Now turn right at the grove of trees. Now take a sharp left."

"Are you sure it wasn't a right turn?" questioned Allan.

"I think he said to turn left. Just keep going," I replied.

Allan dutifully turned left and kept driving. Bethlehem appeared closer and closer. A sheep walked in front of the car, but we assumed it had just strayed away. Soon several shepherds appeared, quizzically looking at us. Next a few chickens scurried in front of the car, along with a typical Bethlehem family, complete with flowing robes and headdresses.

Reality hit the three of us at the same time: "We're driving through Bethlehem!"

Sondra jumped to the floor, telling us she would never recover from this embarrassing experience. She wasn't overreacting—it *was* embarrassing. Here was our little Ford Contour driving down Main Street Bethlehem, carefully avoiding animals, costumed characters and the general public.

"Back up! We haven't gone that far!" I yelled.

With clenched teeth, Allan said, "I can't back up. There are two camels walking behind me."

I advised him to quickly turn left. His response, once more with clenched teeth, was, "If I turn left, I will run over Baby Jesus, sleeping in the manger."

Turning right would have resulted in damage to the "Bethlehem Bakery" tent. We had no choice but to slowly drive down Bethlehem's main drag for one-quarter mile. Normally that's a short distance, but when you're trying to avoid both chickens and a crowd of shepherds, it feels like a cross-country road trip. More than a few shepherds and costumed townspeople made it clear with gestures and facial expressions that we were disrupting the normally tranquil (and motor-less) streets of Bethlehem.

Driving to see Baby Jesus? Well, that's one tradition we've decided not to continue.

And If You Still Don't Believe that Fun Makes a Difference . . .

At Christmas, we have a tradition that makes for interesting pictures. When unwrapping a present, we always remove the bow and stick it on our head. By the end of Christmas morning, we all look as if we're wearing multicolored, sparkling halos. Angels on Christmas morning—not too shabby!

16

Celebrating Wild and Wacky Holidays

The family that plays together, stays together.
ANONYMOUS

Of course your family celebrates all the traditional holidays such as Valentine's Day and Thanksgiving. But have you given much thought to celebrating National Toasted Marshmallow Day on August 30 or Watch a Squirrel Day on October 18?

One year, Sondra went to camp the same week as National Clown Week. A quick trip to the Dollar Store gave me everything I needed to send her a daily package to celebrate this jolly holiday. I mailed clown noses for the girls in her cabin, a three-foot cardboard clown, kazoos and a giant circus poster. When she got home, she admitted, "Mom, the girls in my cabin think you are really cool for celebrating National Clown Week." What greater compliment can a mother get?

In an effort to bring fun and creativity to your family, it's time to make every day a holiday! All right—365 holidays might be a bit much. Still, to give you ideas for each month of the year, instead of the usual Four-Week Program, you're going to get a 12-month program. But don't worry—it's not as much work as it sounds. In fact, you'll be having so much fun, you won't notice that there's been any work involved at all.

Silvana's 12-Month "Let's Get Started Celebrating Untraditional Holidays" Program

January

National Hot Tea Month. Plan a special after-school tea party for your children. Serve cucumber sandwiches and fancy cookies. If your sons balk at the idea of a tea party, tell them you are serving soccer sandwiches. (Cut the bread in circles and serve like a regular sandwich.) In England, children have tea every afternoon, so try to talk in your best British accent.

Take your children to the store and select two or three different flavors of tea. Can they tell the difference between Peppermint and Orange Blossom Mint teas?

Put together a gift basket with various teas, a fancy cup and saucer, and some cookies. Deliver it to a shut-in or your pastor's wife as a special treat.

You can also celebrate:

- January 14: Take a Missionary to Lunch Day
- January 23: National Pie Day
- January 31: Inspire Your Heart with Art Day

February

National Library Lovers' Month. Ask your local library for a "behind the scenes" tour. Kids are fascinated to see the storage areas for excess books. You might even get to see how staff people repair and clean books that have been damaged by customers.

Take your children to the oversized book section. Let them check out some of these heavy books, which are often filled with great photos. A book such as *A Day in the Life of America* provides hours of discussion possibilities as children look at the dynamic photos.

Go through your home library and find books to donate to a children's hospital or women's shelter.

You can also celebrate:

- February 6: Pay a Compliment Day
- February 20: Love Your Pet Day
- February 23: Tootsie Roll Day

March

National Craft Month. Even if you aren't crafty, stop at a craft store and look around. You're sure to find some simple kits to take home and enjoy with your family.

Try an edible craft: Give kids miniature marshmallows and toothpicks. See if they can create squishy sculptures.

Next time you are in the car, pass out an assortment of chenille stems so that kids can make flexible objects. (FYI: The new politically correct term for "pipe cleaners" is now "chenille stems." See what amazing things you learn from this book?)

To inspire creativity, surprise your children with craft-related gifts at breakfast one morning. Wrap up new packages of markers, clay or fancy paper.

You can also celebrate:

- March 2: Dr. Seuss's Birthday
- March 22: National Goof Off Day
- March 26: Make Up Your Own Holiday Day

April

Bedtime Story Month. Plan a special trip to a discount bookstore and let children select a new book to read at bedtime.

Help your children write their own bedtime story. Younger children can dictate the story while you write it out. After they illustrate the story, go to a Kinko's and have their book spiral bound so that it looks like a "real" book.

Do a role reversal at bedtime. Get yourself snuggled in bed early and have children come to you and read while you doze off. (That shouldn't take too long!)

You can also celebrate:

- April 6: National Twinkie Day
- April 21: School Librarian Day
- April 25: Penguin Day

May

Last week in May: *National Backyard Games Week*. Play Hide and Seek in the backyard or at a nearby park. Some kids have actually never played this childhood classic.

Spontaneously round up some neighborhood kids and play Mother May I? and Red Rover, Red Rover. (Do you know some schools have banned Red Rover because they say it's too dangerous?)

Grab some old clothes and have relay races in which team members have to race to dress up in baggy clothes before tagging the next runner.

You can also celebrate:

- May 1: Mother Goose Day
- First Thursday: National Day of Prayer
- May 23: Barney the Dinosaur's Birthday

June

June 7: *National Crayon Day*. Before dinner, ask everyone to dress in one solid color so that they look like a crayon.

Have each family member decorate a pillowcase to help them remember this special holiday. Purchase a package of fabric crayons (they look like regular crayons, yet are designed to create permanent designs on fabric). Color a picture on a piece of paper, using the fabric crayons. Place the paper upside down on a light-colored pillowcase. Follow the package directions to iron the design onto the fabric.

Using crayons, decorate a batch of plain brown lunch bags. That way, each person gets a designer bag to make his or her lunch special.

You can also celebrate:

- June 1: National Barefoot Day
- June 9: Donald Duck's Birthday
- June 24: Eat Cereal Day
- June 27: Paul Bunyan Day

July

National Picnic Month. Invite friends over for a potluck picnic. Tell people to bring food that begins with the same letter as their last name—the Clarks bring cookies while the Petersons bring potato salad.

If a pond or lake is nearby, teach children how to skip rocks. It's fun to watch a flat rock "skip" over the water.

Don't worry if it rains on the day of your picnic. Put the gingham tablecloth on the living room floor and pretend you're outside. Gather all the houseplants around the tablecloth—all the greenery will convince your guests they are really outside.

Plan an ethnic picnic. Serve a variety of foods from other countries. Barbecue meat for Mexican *carne asada* or skewer mini-meatballs for an Italian favorite.

You can also celebrate:

- July 7: Father/Daughter Take a Walk Day
- July 10: Teddy Bear's Picnic Day
- July 11: Cheer Up the Lonely Day

August

Second week in August: *National Apple Week*. Plan to have an old-fashioned apple-bobbing contest. Fill a tub with apples and time each other to see who is fastest when it comes to grabbing an apple with their teeth.

Check to see if local orchards offer you-pick apples. Kids enjoy getting fresh apples right off the tree.

Purchase a variety of different apples. Slice each apple and label it: "Golden Delicious," "Granny Smith" or "Fuji." Have family members taste each variety. Vote to determine your family favorite.

You can also celebrate:

- First Sunday: Sister's Day
- August 10: National Garage Sale Day
- August 29: Mary Poppins's Birthday

September

National Breakfast Month. Make sure children are hungry for breakfast. Pick one day this month to wake everyone up an hour early for a brisk bike ride or walk before breakfast. They'll be eager to come home and eat a healthy meal.

See if your children can figure out these egg-related puns. What word is created by adding the two words together?

+ = **Explain**

+ = **Exchange**

+ = **Exit**

Pick a morning when you have extra time to have a formal breakfast. Add a festive atmosphere by lighting the candles, digging out the good china and eating breakfast in the dining room. But be sure to still wear clean pajamas instead of tuxedos!

You can also celebrate:

- September 9: Party Party Day
- September 18: National Play Dough Day
- September 29: National Pumpkin Day

October

Popcorn Popping Month. Buy some colored popcorn at your grocery store. Have children guess whether the popped popcorn will also be multicolored. Then pop it to find out.

Set up a mini-baseball game in your house. The batter holds a spatula as the pitcher tosses a piece of popped popcorn over the plate.

When the children are out of the room, make a batch of microwave popcorn and a batch of stove-popped popcorn. Can your children tell the difference?

You can also celebrate:

- October 8: National Silly Day
- October 15: National Grouch Day
- October 22: National Pretzel Day

November

Sunday to Sunday of Thanksgiving Week: *National Bible Week*. Dress up as Bible characters. Old bathrobes and sheets work fine for Moses, Jonah or David costumes. Your toddler can bring out his fuzzy pajamas and be a sheep on the Ark.

Gather all the Bibles in your house and give one to each family member. Select a psalm to read. Taking turns, have each family member read aloud the psalm from his or her version of the Bible. Which translation is easiest to understand? Which version conveys a message that is slightly different from that of the others?

Collect all the loose change in your house. Use the money to buy a new Bible for someone in the community who doesn't have one.

You can also celebrate:

- November 3: National Sandwich Day
- November 15: Clean Out Your Refrigerator Day
- November 17: Homemade Bread Day

December

National Stress-Free Holidays Month. Avoid the stress of the holidays by telling your children to make a list of their must-have Christmas gifts. The only catch: The list can feature only five items. If they absolutely have to have a particular item, they may need to drop something else from the list. You'll be surprised at how the list changes from day to day. (Definitely set a deadline for when the final version is due on Santa's desk.)

Who says you have to spend hours baking delicate holiday cookies that require hours of preparation? Find a good bakery and buy the desserts you need.

Put all the wrapping supplies in a box or basket. Include wrapping paper, tape, gift bags, tissue paper, gift tags, ribbons and marking pens. That way, when someone needs to wrap presents, all the necessary supplies are in one place. Now that's a good idea!

You can also celebrate:

- December: Read a New Book Month
- December 20: National Exercise Day
- December 22: Flashlight Day

Have you been inspired by all the ways you can celebrate? Never have a boring, ordinary day again!

If you're motivated to celebrate even more holidays, check out my book *Every Day a Holiday*, where I outline activities and share craft and snack ideas related to over 320 holidays. You can get more help with untraditional holidays from the following websites:

- www.brownielocks.com
- www.chases.com
- www.holidays.net

Ask the Fun Consultant

Silvana, these ideas sound fun, but I don't have time to find kazoos for National Kazoo Day or paint the driveway to look like a yellow brick road for Wizard of Oz Day. How can I celebrate without a big budget or hours of preparation?

Good question! These holidays are supposed to be fun, not labor-intensive. How about trying some of these ideas?

- Designate a box or drawer to be "The Holiday Box." When you see a bag of plastic pumpkins on sale in January at a craft store for 70-percent off, buy them for The Holiday Box to use in October. One mom went to a PTA luncheon where the tables were decorated with silver stars. She saw the clean-up committee start to toss the stars, so she quickly collected them to put in her Holiday Box. The 200 stars soon found themselves incorporated into festivities for Barney's Birthday and as awards for National Read-A-Book Month. Any time you find something a bit out of the ordinary, toss it in The Holiday Box. Even an old "Happy New Year" sign can be changed to "Happy New Toothbrush Day."

• Remember that a small prop goes a long way with a child's imagination. On Wizard of Oz Day, simply cover a bike helmet with aluminum foil, wear a grey sweatshirt and tell your children you are the Tin Man. On National Penguin Day, dress in black and white and waddle like a penguin while serving breakfast.

• Mealtime is a natural place to celebrate these untraditional holidays. Of course you'll add green food coloring to your scrambled eggs on Dr. Suess's Birthday. Don't forget to serve a picnic on the floor in honor of Teddy Bear's Picnic or give children their own yeast dough on National Pretzel Day to make their own pretzels.

And If You Still Don't Believe that Fun Makes a Difference . . .

We hear so much about creating positive memories for our children. What better way to give your child some warm, fuzzy feelings about his or her childhood? It may be a drizzling, windy, hard-to-get-out-of-bed morning, yet if your child is greeted in the bathroom with a sign saying "Happy National Twinkie Day!" and sees you dressed in beige (to look like a giant Twinkie), the day looks brighter. Naturally, you'll throw nutrition warnings aside and serve Twinkies for breakfast. Who can beat that for a memory?

Don't hesitate to make up your own holiday. Last week as we drove to church, my husband announced that today was a very special holiday: It was Crazy Costco Day. With that, he handed Sondra and me coupons that read: "Celebrate Crazy Costco Day with this $50.00 coupon for the items of your choice." Of course, after church, we headed to Costco, celebrating a holiday that the store doesn't even know exists!

17

Travel Is Terrific!

The World is a book, and those who do not travel read only a page.

St. Augustine

Glancing at the school calendar, I shouted, "Great! There's no school next Monday. Where can we go?"

In our home, "Where can we go?" is our family motto. We'll take any chance to go anywhere, anytime. Once we flew to Africa on Christmas Eve because airfare was so cheap we couldn't pass it up. Another time I saw a small advertisement in the paper offering an incredible all-inclusive package including airfare, hotel and ski passes for 12 days in Austria. Never one to turn down a bargain, I quickly signed our family up. I did, however, overlook the fine print, which said that the package included a 24-hour, round-trip bus ride from the Austrian airport to the ski resort. As an added bonus, the double-decker bus carried 45 drinking, partying, wild-and-crazy Italian college students on the top deck. But, hey, that's what travel is all about. We still got more than our money's worth from that travel experience.

People sometimes ask, "Why do you feel travel is so important?"

Ah, why do we travel? Let me count the ways:

Travel helps us see that not everyone lives the way we do

Relatives who live in St. Mary's, Iowa, enjoy their town with a population of 436. Sondra was thrilled to walk down the middle of their main street, knowing that any car coming by would slow down for her. Visiting our agent, who lives in an apartment on Fifth Avenue in Manhattan, opened our eyes to a way of life with tiny kitchens and no need to own a car. On Bugala Island in Uganda, our family visited a group home for AIDS orphans. After distributing some markers, paper and craft supplies to the children, I looked for a wastebasket to toss away some trash. Imagine my surprise to discover the group home had no need of a wastebasket. Every scrap piece of paper was recycled, and nothing came in plastic shrinkwrap, in cans or in anything else that needed to be discarded.

Travel gives children confidence for handling new experiences
It takes skill to find the correct gate at the airport terminal. How do you exchange money in a foreign country? What do you do when a waitress in Tennessee asks if you want "meat and three"? ("Meat and three" means a meat dish with three sides of potatoes, vegetables, fries, rice or stuffing.) All these new experiences stretch children and give them survival skills. They learn how to ask for help and how to figure things out on their own. At first, the multicolored lines of a New York subway map look like senseless squiggles. With a little research, however, the S Line and the P Line make sense and get you where you need to go. And if a 12-year-old can figure out a New York subway map, he or she can surely figure out how to change classes on the first day of middle school.

Travel gives us an awareness of God's amazing creativity
Living in the Pacific Northwest made us familiar with lush ferns, the San Juan Islands and the infamous Mount St. Helens. What a contrast from never needing an umbrella at the Grand Canyon! We've been fortunate to see the dry, barren landscape outside Lima, Peru, in contrast with the forest surrounding Machu Picchu. In Texas, we joined the locals in their recreational activities: We sat on plastic discs and slid down 40-foot

sand dunes. All these new places and people allow for meaningful conversation about how and why people live where they do.

Travel draws families together

Shopping for socks at the local Wal-Mart isn't anything special. Shopping for bread in a Mexican bakery suddenly gives us a new experience to share. We have to select the bread, figure out how much it costs, decide how to pay and use whatever Spanish we know to make ourselves understood. Suddenly the simple act of going to a bakery creates a family memory. On a cold and rainy night, our family ordered a large pizza in Cuzco, Peru. Thinking about the poor children who were begging outside our restaurant, I limited my family to one piece of pizza each. We distributed the leftover pizza to grateful children. Now, whenever we eat pizza, we have a greater appreciation for the abundance of food available to us.

For some families, the idea of traveling is a daunting proposition, as they consider packing, arranging transportation, dealing with cranky kids, lost plane tickets, missed nap times, picky eaters, crowded hotel rooms, overpriced restaurants and unfamiliar territory. Here come some practical tips to the rescue. By the time you complete this Four-Week "Let's Get Started Traveling" Program, you'll be ready to hit the road (airport, train station or bus line).

Silvana's Four-Week "Let's Get Started Traveling" Program

Week One

Do some research about day trips near your house. Check out your city's website and see if there's a link to "Day Trips." Often, local Chambers of Commerce offer insight into attractions a short distance from home. Find two or three options and discuss them with your family. Do they want to visit a pretzel factory to see how the dough gets shaped into pretzels, or head off in the opposite direction and go through a corn maze? Offer several options, and then have family members vote to decide where you'll go.

Week Two

Go! That's right—go to the location you selected last week. Start small. There's no need to make a marathon drive of 300 miles in one day. Take a casual drive to the pretzel factory, and make sure to stop at any park or other attraction along the way. Remember to enjoy the process of traveling, appreciating new experiences rather than accumulating miles on the car. After reaching your destination, have a picnic or special ice-cream treat. No need to break the budget. Many kids are happy knowing they can order ice cream at Dairy Queen.

Week Three

Congratulations! You survived a day trip. Now it's time to move on to an overnight trip. Once again, contact your local Chamber of Commerce or get a book from the library on nearby attractions. Many books are available with titles such as *Day Trips from Nashville*, *Day Trips from Seattle*, *Day Trips from Chicago* . . . get the idea?

Kids get excited when you let them help decide where you'll go. Often, a hotel with a swimming pool is all they need to be happy. Or check out www.childrensmuseums.org together to find some great interactive museums your family might visit. Looking for something a bit more unique than a museum? Visit www.roadsideamerica.com, which describes hundreds of offbeat tourist attractions ranging from "shoe trees" (trees covered with at least 50 pairs of shoes), to underground tunnels for frogs to travel across busy streets, to the world's largest cherry-pie pans. Just punch in where you live, and the website lets you know about some one-of-a-kind attraction in your area. (What family near Austin, Minnesota, wouldn't want to visit the SPAM® Museum to participate in a SPAM-carving contest?)

Week Four

Time to take off on your overnight travel adventure. Load up the car and set out on a family mini-vacation. Be flexible. Don't forget: The idea is to enjoy new experiences together. Remember Chevy Chase's movie *National Lampoon's Family Vacation*? Even though you're still fairly close to home, act like tourists. Take pictures in front of your hotel. Get postcards and send them to Grandma (even though she lives 25 miles away). Buy an inexpensive souvenir of your trip.

Did you survive? Let's hope that this Four-Week Program was just the start of many new family travel adventures.

Ask the Fun Consultant

Silvana, I like the idea of short family trips, but my kids drive me crazy in the car. How can I stop all that backseat squabbling? I don't think I can stand another "Mom, Emma's looking at me!"

Don't let your kids' petty arguments prevent you from traveling. Here are some ways to make car rides enjoyable.

- Who says Dad drives while Mom plays referee? Switch roles. Let Mom drive and put Dad in charge of playing countless games of I Spy. Better yet, let a child over 12 take a turn sitting in the front seat (passenger side, of course). An adult in the back automatically cuts down on sibling fights.

· Have family devotions in the car using a new family devotional.

· Give each child a see-through hanging shoe bag. The bag hangs from the back of the front seat and stores all the kiddie paraphernalia essential for successful car travel. Children can store markers, small toys, cards, books, and so on.

· Ahead of time, find a roadmap of the route you are taking. Make copies so that each child can follow the landmarks on the map and more fully enjoy the trip.

· Make a rule: Children cannot ask, "Are we there yet?" If they want to say those words, they have to sing them with a made-up tune.

· Avoid stopping for lunch at sit-down restaurants. Instead, let children play for 30 to 40 minutes at a local park or McDonald's-type indoor playground. After they're done exercising, eat while driving in the car. This helps pass another half hour or so as kids eat and relax from their fun.

· Wrap up an assortment of small new toys. Designate these the 50-Mile or 100-Mile Surprises. After driving the designated number of miles, well-behaved children get a gift.

· Bring along jump ropes or soccer balls to use at rest stops. Ten minutes jumping rope equals 20 minutes of "almost silence" from the back seat. Try running some races from one end of the rest stop to the other.

Okay, Silvana, but where should we go?

Now that your children are entertained in the back seat, it's time to find some places to visit. The Internet has a wealth of resources. Just looking at these websites will get you inspired to start packing:

- www.travelingmom.com
- www.familytraveltimes.com
- www.familytravelforum.com
- www.travelwithkids.com
- www.family-friendlyvacations.com

You're sure to find something that appeals to your family—there's something for every interest and budget.

Hostels

Speaking of budgets, have you ever considered staying in a hostel? If you were one of those 1970s-backpacking-through-Europe-on-$5-a-day hippies, relax—many of today's hostels are geared toward families and "mature" adults. In fact, the Youth Hostel Association has officially dropped the word "Youth" and is now known as Hostelling International. Check out www.hihostels.com.

While hostels are more prevalent overseas, many exist in the United States. For a reasonable price, your family stays in a clean, safe facility where noise is tolerated. Travelers of all ages and parts of the world stay at hostels for the reasonable cost as well as the casual atmosphere. No need to tell your children "Please be quiet" or "Don't touch that antique vase!" Breakfast is also included in the price, making hostels a real bargain.

Here are a few hostels located in the United States:

- Stay in an actual teepee on Vashon Island, Washington.

- Stay in Hollywood at the Banana Bungalow Hostel, which offers shuttle service between its facility and southern California tourist attractions. The 250-bed hostel features a pool, restaurant, theater and parking. Other locations are in Miami, Santa Barbara and San Diego.

- Try the Big Apple Hostel in downtown New York, located right in Times Square. You'll get a basic clean room with access to a laundry and kitchen. Best of all, your family will meet intrepid travelers from all over the world.

Back to Camp

If hostels aren't your style, consider taking the whole family to camp. Yes, camp. More and more families find all-inclusive camps an ideal way to guarantee that their vacation will include age-appropriate activities for everyone. Meals are included, so even Mom gets a chance to relax. And don't worry about sleeping in decrepit cabins swarming with bugs. Many of these family camps offer first-class accommodations.

Check out these camps:

- One of the most established family camp programs is sponsored by YMCA of the Rockies in Colorado. See www.ymcarockies.org for more details.

- Pine Cove Summer Camps offer a wide range of activities in a Christian setting. See www.pinecove.com/familycamps for further information.

- I spent several summers at Forest Home Christian Conference Center and can vouch for their high-quality family camps. Check out www.foresthome.org to see what they have to offer.

- If your family likes performing or being involved in fine arts, try Cazadero Performing Arts Camp. See www.cazadero.org for more information.

Family Fun on Any Budget

Now that you've conquered close-to-home travel, it's time to move on. Here are a few places that offer great family vacations for all interests and all budgets.

- Jekyll Island Club Hotel is located on an island off the coast of Georgia. Enjoy special family vacation packages that include supervised children's activities and a first-class playground. In addition, families can explore 10 miles of beach, ride horses and visit the Georgia Sea Turtle Center. Twenty miles of paved trails lets the family enjoy safe bike riding. Canoes and kayaks are available to explore the inland waterways. No chance of being bored! Check out www.jekyllisland.com or call (912) 635-3636.

- Like the outdoors? The Snowbird Ski and Summer Resort in Utah has it all, all year round. In the winter, kids under age six ski free. You can also enjoy snowmobiling, tubing and snowshoeing. Summer activities include a 1,000-foot zip line, an alpine slide, aerial trams and musical events. See www.snowbird.com.

- Ever watched the *Today Show* and wondered about all those people who stand outside the studio waving at the cameras? They are all tourists in New York! Don't be intimidated by the rumors of rough and tough New Yorkers—our family visits at least once a year, and we feel safer in New York than we do in our small hometown. Everything falls into place once you find the right place to stay. Maps, signs and brochures help you easily find any attraction. And there's no need to rent a car because buses and subways take you everywhere. Try these family-friendly hotels:

> Affinia Hotels offer nine locations in the city. The all-suites rooms come with mini-refrigerators, ideal for families wanting to save on the cost of meals. In addition, they offer American Girl Packages, complete with a bed for your daughter's American Girl doll. A Fun-for-Family chest is stocked with games and arts-and-crafts supplies when children need some quiet time from all that New York has to offer. Check out www.affinia.com or call (212) 465-3700.

> Carnegie Suites are ideal for families—they offer a great location as well as a full kitchenette with microwave and refrigerator. The complimentary breakfast is an easy way to get a start on the day when you visit this fast-paced city. See www.carnegiehotel.com.

• We've been fortunate to travel to many countries, yet Seattle is still one of our favorite places to visit. Just last month we spent the weekend at the Alexis Hotel (www.alexishotel.com), located within walking distance of many attractions. We kept the cost low by strolling to Pike Street Market for breakfast (passing the original Starbucks location), checking out special events near the Space Needle at the Seattle Center, and walking along the waterfront. On other trips, we've enjoyed Seattle's fantastic children's museum, kayaking on Lake Union (past the houseboat where *Sleepless in Seattle* was filmed) and watching boats at the Ballard Locks.

• Our family had a great time visiting St. Augustine, Florida, the oldest city in America, where we stayed about 20 minutes south at the Ginn Hammock Beach

Resort. Ah, this was the good life! When we arrived, a staff person gave us a personal tour. The three of us had more than enough space in our one-bedroom unit, which was more like an apartment than a hotel room. The resort offers indoor and outdoor pools, along with a supervised and well-planned Kid's Crew program. The Jack Nicklaus Ocean Hammock Golf Course runs parallel to the ocean. We found the staff exceptionally friendly and the facilities sparkling clean. Check out online at www.hammockbeach.com or call (386) 246-5580.

> If you are on a super-tight budget, consider switching homes with friends who live close by. Many families do this as a way to feel they are "getting away from it all" when really they are just 20 miles away. The experience allows you to feel like you've been on a vacation because you are visiting new parks, new local swimming pools and even a new McDonald's!

- Want something just a bit more adventurous? Check out hundreds of vacation opportunities sponsored by Backroads. This adventure touring company was voted one of the top tour operators by *Travel & Leisure* magazine. Just looking through their catalog will have you drooling over your suitcases. Choose from family-oriented trips ranging from a safari in Africa to hiking and biking in Yosemite. Check out online at www.backroads.com or call (800) 462-2848.

- Does your family enjoy skiing? How about a visit to the Yellowstone area, where you can ski at the Grand Targhee Resort? In addition to skiing, the resort offers dog sledding, nature-based kids' camps and ice skating. The nursery is state licensed, so you can feel comfortable leaving your babies. Check out www.grand targhee.com or call (307) 353-2300.

- How about a family-oriented kayak trip? Sea Kayak Adventures, Inc. has operated sea kayak tours to the premier whale watching destinations of Baja California in Mexico and in Vancouver Island, British Columbia, since 1993. Blue and fin whales are frequently seen in the Sea of Cortez on the Baja sea kayaking tours, while you can paddle with orcas near Robson Bite Orca Preserve, a biological wonderland between mainland British Columbia and Vancouver Island. The camping, whale watching and sea kayaking BC Canada trips feature close encounters with wildlife, whales, extraordinary wilderness areas and incredible cuisine. No prior experience is necessary and they provide all the equipment needed. Check out their family trips on www.seakayakadventures.com or call (800) 616-1943.

- If you like visiting National Parks, Zion Mountain Resort is the ideal solution. Located at the gate of Zion National Park in Utah, the resort is in the midst of North America's highest concentration of natural scenic wonders, with easy access to Zion National Park, Bryce Canyon, the Grand Canyon's North Rim, Lake Powell and Grand Staircase National Monument. Your family can enjoy guided horseback rides, mountain biking, mountaineering, rock climbing or an archaeological tour. Kids will enjoy spotting a free-roaming herd of buffalo, migrating herds of mule deer, wild turkeys and other wildlife. Visit www.zionmountainre sort.com or call (435) 688-7722 for more information.

Europe, Here We Come!

If you're ready to head out of the country, consider taking a tour with Rick Steves. His "Family Europe in 14 Days" tour covers Florence, Paris, Tuscany and even Neuschwanstein Castle. All breakfasts are included. I love the tour's motto: "Great guides, small groups, no grumps!" Many other European tours are available also. Watch just one of his travel shows on PBS, and you'll be racing to pack your suitcase. Check out www.rick steves.com or call (425) 771-8303.

Landal GreenParks have 59 locations throughout Europe. The parks have family bungalows that are childproof and equipped with everything you need for a carefree vacation. Kids' activities allow parents to get a break also. Most parks are located in Holland, meaning you'll have plenty of chances for flat, safe bike rides. Check out www.landalgreenparks.com.

Center Parcs allow you to rent cabins or apartments in 16 locations throughout Europe. The "parks" offer fully equipped lodging along with restaurants, pools and activities. Children's programs include wave pools, pony riding, indoor playgrounds, jungle expeditions and high adventure activities. A great way to spend a family vacation where kids can be noisy! Check out www.centerparcs.com.

Sometimes a tour that takes care of all those pesky travel details is a great bargain. Tourcrafters arranges your flights from the U.S. to major cities like Vienna, Paris, Rome and Madrid. Tourcrafters will match their tours with your family's needs. How does a tour through Italy by train sound? Perhaps you'd like an escorted tour through the French and Italian Riviera. Contact www.tourcrafters.com to find a trip for you and your family.

Sun and Beach Fun

But what if Europe isn't your idea of a great vacation? What if you'd rather be sunning yourself on a beach instead of running around cobblestone streets and visiting museums? Never fear, other warm options are here.

Beaches Resorts offer families all-inclusive programs in the Caribbean. You don't even have to carry a purse to the pool! If your children want ice cream or a snack, it's all included in the price. Also included are water sports, all meals, great rooms and suites, scuba diving, and even tips. Beaches offers trained staff to lead quality children's programs. You relax (or scuba dive) while your children have fun with energetic counselors. Beaches Resorts are the only Caribbean destinations where you'll find a colorful cast of characters including Elmo, Cookie Monster, Grover, Zoe, Bert and Ernie, and now Abby Cadabby. Throughout the day, kids can enjoy the Caribbean Adventure with Sesame Street® with a full schedule of events. Check out www.beaches.com or call (888) BEACHES.

Riu Hotels specialize in sun and sand holidays with locations in Mexico, the Bahamas, Miami, Costa Rica, and around the world. Half of their hotels are all-inclusive, which means you don't have to worry about airport transfers and children's programs. Visit www.riu.com.

Want to spend some time on an island? Try Coconut Bay Resort on St. Lucia. The 254-room resort lets you choose from the pool, the ocean or the spa. For kids, there's the Cocoland Kids' Club with fun and educational activities led by trained and enthusiastic counselors. Check out www.coconutbayresort andspa.com.

Want something a little more exotic? Check out Thompson Family Adventures if you think a trip to Belize, China, Peru or Costa Rica would appeal to your family. You'll have a deluxe tour and your kids get matched up with an overseas pen pal to develop a cross-cultural relationship. Thompson Family Adventures schedules tours around school vacations and provides free travel insurance. They've recently added a new tour to Portugal and offer several tours geared for families with teens. Just think: a vacation where teens are actively engaged and not complaining about missing their cell phone! Visit www.familyad ventures.com or call (800) 262-6255.

And If You Still Don't Believe that Fun Makes a Difference . . .

Travel experiences aren't always as carefree as brochures portray. Sondra and I were once strolling down a street in Cuzco, Peru, and I had a backpack filled with baby clothes to give to some of the begging women we had seen earlier in the day. Rounding a corner on a deserted street, we saw a weary-looking pregnant woman sitting in the dust with a toddler. I casually knelt next to her and gestured if she wanted the two or three baby items in my hand. Out of nowhere, we were suddenly surrounded by 10 or 15 women, literally grabbing baby clothes from my backpack. I didn't care about the clothes, but knew my wallet and passport were on the bottom. I tried to get up, but couldn't move because of the women pressing against me, groping inside my pack.

Suddenly Sondra grabbed my arm and pulled me up and we ran down the street, followed by the women. I tossed all the clothes on the ground, and we raced into the safety of a souvenir shop.

Not your typical tourist travel activity, but I'm sure your family vacation will not be quite so exciting. By doing your homework and planning ahead, you'll find a place where your entire family can rest, relax and just enjoy being together. So get busy with those travel brochures and let the vacation planning begin!

A Final Word

Now that you've had your entire family life turned 180 degrees from what is described in traditional parenting books, how do you feel? How do you feel about your family? It's my hope that you and your kids are closer than ever—and that you are realizing that family life can be so much more than just day-to-day routines.

Remember, whether it's helping kids with homework or showing them how to load the dishwasher, a lighthearted spirit and sense of humor go a long way. Your kids just want you to spend time with them—and to enjoy yourself in the process. By using the tips in this book in the days and years to come, you can ensure that your family will go on loving and laughing together.

Happy parenting!

About the Author

When not writing books, Silvana Clark is a professional speaker who presents business-related keynotes and workshops across the United States, Canada and overseas. Some of her most requested topics include:

Marketing with a Big Imagination and a Small Budget
Creativity: What Is It and Where Do I Get It?
Humor in the Workplace
Surviving Change with a Camera in Your Face

In her non-professional life, Silvana trained her dog to star in TV commercials, spent a year traveling around the United States in an RV and appeared on the Fox reality show *Trading Spouses*. She's happiest when every day is completely different from the day before.

If you want to see her *really* happy, just watch her any time she is traveling with her family. (And don't tell anyone, but Silvana and her family frequently visit hotels and resorts as "mystery guests" to report on the service they receive. You'll never recognize them because they wear elaborate disguises like plastic mustaches and florescent wigs.)

Check out her website at www.silvanaclark.com.